The Great American
Book Musical

Also by Denny Martin Flinn

Ready for My Close-up: Great Movie Speeches

Little Musicals for Little Theatres: A Guide to the Musicals That Don't Need Chandeliers and Helicopters to Succeed

How Not to Audition

How Not to Write a Screenplay

Musical! A Grand Tour: The Rise, Glory and Fall of an American Institution

What They Did for Love: The Story of the Making of the Broadway musical A Chorus Line

The Fearful Summons (a *Star Trek* novel)

San Francisco Kills

Killer Finish

Star Trek VI: The Undiscovered Country (with Nicholas Meyer, a screenplay)

The Great American Book Musical

A Manifesto
A Monograph
A Manual

Denny Martin Flinn

Limelight Editions
An Imprint of Hal Leonard Corporation
New York

Published in 2008 by Limelight Editions
An Imprint of Hal Leonard Corporation
7777 West Bluemound Road
Milwaukee, WI 53213

Trade Book Division Editorial Offices
19 West 21st Street, New York, NY 10010

Grateful acknowledgment is made to the following for permission to use previously published materials:

Abrams Artists Agency, on behalf of the Estates of Peter Stone and Sherman Edwards: Excerpt from *1776*. Used by permission.

Eric Olsen: Excerpt from "Spring Awakening" by Randall A. Byrn, Blogcritics.org (July 22, 2006). Used by permission.

Gary DaSilva, on behalf of Neil Simon: Excerpt from *Promises, Promises*. Used by permission.

Robinson, Brog, Leinwand, Greene, Genovese, and Gluck, on behalf of Jerry Bock, Sheldon Harnick, and the Estates of Jerome Weidman and George Abbott: Excerpt from *Fiorello!* Used by permission.

Printed in the United States of America

Book design by Snow Creative Services

Library of Congress Cataloging-in-Publication Data
   Flinn, Denny Martin.
   The great American book musical : a manifesto, a monograph, a manual / by Denny Martin Flinn.
      p. cm.
   Includes bibliographical references.
   ISBN 978-0-87910-362-0 (pbk.)
      1. Musicals—United States—History and criticism. I. Title.
   ML1711.F56 2008
   792.60973—dc22

                         2008039958

www.limelighteditions.com

To Rodney Strong,
who taught me to dance,
and Ken Bachtold,
who told me to choreograph

Contents

Preface

I had a great deal of trouble with the subtitle for this book. Is it a manifesto, "a public declaration of principles"? Certainly I propose principles here that are not generally held (e.g., only choreographers should direct musicals). A monograph, "a scholarly piece of writing . . . on a specific, often limited subject"? As it is my contention that what I define as the great American book musical is an art form pretty much of the past, the subject of this book could hardly be more specific or limited. As for a "how-to" manual, "a small reference book, especially one giving instructions" (*American Heritage Dictionary*), it is unlikely that, with only this book in hand, the reader could write, produce, direct, or choreograph a musical. Nevertheless, I hope that by investigating what made the best musicals so entertaining, anyone pursuing the cause might benefit.

So I chose all three, in the event that the casual browser might be intrigued, and be encouraged to purchase.

Here I have tried to define what made the greatest of Broadway musicals great, first by tracing the development of the integration of musical techniques, and then by examining the contribution of libretto, music, lyrics, and staging to the most successful musicals.

When, as a teenager, I saw my first Broadway musicals, they drew me into their worlds completely. It did not occur to me that there were parts to the whole. Over the years of an eclectic career in theatre, I discovered and admired those parts. Of course, the very success of a great American book musical—that is, a story told through scene, song, and dance—is in the disappearance of those parts back into the whole. You probably shouldn't visit the kitchen of a great restaurant. (Believe me. I was a waiter once.) So if you love musicals but only want to see them, don't go backstage. And don't read this book.

But if you'd like to know more, I hope this small manifesto, monograph, or manual will help.

—DMF

Prologue

"Any great work of art . . . revives and readapts time and space, and the measure of its success is the extent to which it makes you an inhabitant of that world—the extent to which it invites you in and lets you breathe its strange, special air."
—Leonard Bernstein, *The Joy of Music*

What Is the Great American Book Musical?

During the first half of the twentieth century, as the Provincetown Players, Eugene O'Neill, the Group Theatre, the Actor's Studio, and others established realism and naturalism in playwrighting and acting, the door was opened for drama that was able to catch not just the fancy but the emotions of the audience. Even the great theatrical works of the past, by the Greeks, Shakespeare, Molière, are performed differently today than they were in their time. We now go to the theatre not just to admire the rhetoric, the bombast, the sword fights, the costumes, and the romantic, poetic, and melodramatic, but to suspend our disbelief, to enter a rare, parallel universe, different from our own lives, yet so meaningful to them. Though certainly the playwrights of the past strove to entertain us, surely it became easier when the technique of the actors became more allied with their character's reality than with the declamations and postures of the performer.

Musical entertainments followed that same path, slowly but inevitably.

In the attempt to remain faithful to his character, the actor only had to portray the truth. The singer and the dancer found that more difficult, due to the heightened theatricality of their work. They required a wholesale rewriting of the kind of musical entertainment that had endeared them to audiences for thousands of years.

It had all started in earnest with Richard Wagner, the German grand opera composer who in 1849 first used the term *gesamtkunstwerk*, variously translated as a "universal," "complete," "total," or "unified" work of art. Wagner, a lifelong theatre lover who wrote his own lyrics, directed many of his own productions, and eventually built his own theatre (thank you, King Ludwig), held that all the techniques of the theatre should reinforce the drama. Each element should serve the story. Also in Germany, the Duke of Saxe-Meiningen (1826–1914), now considered the father of the modern director—that is, the first to make it a separate occupation—created his own theatre company with the desire to make all the elements blend in support of the drama. In England, the designer and theatre theorist Edward Gordon Craig wrote that "the Art of the Theatre is neither acting nor the play, it is not scene nor dance, but it consists of all the elements of which these things are composed . . . " (*On the Art of the Theatre*, 1911, revised 1957).

On the American musical stage, this finally, fully came about in 1943 with *Oklahoma!*, when its choreographer used a dance vocabulary that was suggested by the characters, and created a dance sequence—the famous "Dream Ballet"—that delved into the psychology of the heroine. Until then, most dance in musicals had been of the "bring-on-the-girls" variety.

So the American book musical arrived when its writers began to insist that the dialogue be realistic—even jokes should derive from character—and that the songs and dances should help forward the plot, sound native to the time and place of the setting, and derive from the psychology of the characters. And the American book musical truly arrived when these various techniques flowed smoothly in and out of each other.

All that, without giving up the scintillating entertainment of song and dance.

There are many valid musical theatre forms besides the book musical: operetta (*A Light in the Piazza*), rock opera (*The Who's Tommy*), poperetta (*Jesus Christ Superstar*), rockeretta (*Rent*), dance (*Movin' Out, Contact, Dancin'*), jukebox or catalogue musicals (*Smokey Joe's Cafe, Jersey Boys*), plays with music (*Blood Brothers*), and good old-fashioned musical comedy (*No, No, Nanette; 42nd Street*), all entertaining, commercial, and important to the health of the theatre. Peter Brook once called Broadway the greatest experimental theatre in the world, because of its acceptance of such a wide range of material. But American musical entertainment reached an apotheosis of brilliance in the form of the book musical. Other forms may be just as interesting; none are as native American. Other forms may be just as entertaining; none are as dramatic.

The American book musical, then, is a drama—or tragedy, comedy, or farce—presented through the elements of dialogue, lyrics, and dance, all woven together to create the seamless presentation of a story.

That "woven together" is the key. Though in *Oklahoma!* dancers replaced the actors playing Curly and Laurey for the "Dream Ballet," soon afterward the unique American musical comedy performer arrived, he and she who could sing, dance, and act. Authors soon came to learn that the triple-threat performer was available, and wrote not down to the talents of the cast, but up to the rigors of the role.

And there it is. Each plot point told, each character expressing his ideas and actions, within the technique that best communicates those story elements. All rolled together so that the audience, when the musical theatre is at its best, barely notices the technique. At a great performance of a great American book musical, the audience should be so involved in the drama that they are unaware of the shift from scene to song to dance.

When *A Chorus Line* opened, several critics, used to the "chorus" being trotted out for showstopping dance numbers, remarked on the irony that a musical about dancers held so little actual dancing, an epic misunderstanding in that *A Chorus Line* was strictly choreographed from curtain to curtain, its staging so integrated, support for the emotional ideas so complete, that the choreography was indivisible from the text.

The slickness, the attention to detail, and the precision with which American musicals were staged is the very essence of the form, different by far than British theatre. It is an American trait, this perfectionism, this straining for the next improvement, and it informs our culture, our business, our very lives. Onstage, it created the great American book musical.

Why a Book About It?

Because, like cave paintings and Impressionism, it's over. Live theatre will never die. Broadway may last for years as a clearinghouse for the most commercial musical entertainments. But the art of the American book musical has already metamorphosed into something other than what years of work by writers and choreographers had created: the seamless, integrated, dramatic (or comedic) musical.

Museums keep historical styles of art before the public. Hopefully theatres will keep the book musical alive. New generations may yet thrill to reproductions of the great shows created throughout the twentieth century, and perhaps even new versions in the format. After all, someone is still writing opera. But as time goes by, theatre owners may not fully understand what they are producing. Directors and choreographers, trying to reinvent the wheel, will throw out the baby with the bathwater. I'm trying here to leave a record of the technique, to create a blueprint for an ancient art.

What seems to be missing from the American theatre today (in both plays and musicals) is creativity. It isn't just the recent "Disneyfication" or "corporatization" of Broadway—words many critics have used to decry the safe, brand-name, by-the-numbers pop musical entertainments or the lugubrious, cheaply executed revivals that proliferate on Broadway today. It's an across-the-board failure of the directorial imagination. Where "concepts" exist, they often interfere with, rather than support, the text. Call that the Peter Sellars school of theatre—let's set *The Oresteia* in a delicatessen! (Sellars, recipient of a MacArthur Foundation "genius grant," had to be replaced during his only attempt at a Broadway musical.)

True creative imagination finds a unique approach that furthers our interest in, and understanding of, the story while being, certainly in the case of musicals, extremely entertaining. Pseudo-music (all complex forms and high notes); dances that feature steps everyone recognizes from beginning tap, jazz, and ballet classes; a lack of originality in lyric ideas; sets and costumes featuring little beyond authenticity; adaptations of great films that add nothing and lose much; and revivals that look more like the theatrical period in which the show was first produced than the historical period the show takes place in have all conspired to obscure the dazzling, theatrical nature of the original American book musical.

I should reveal that, having grown up in the musical theatre as a dancer, I have a prejudice toward the staging. Some may define the golden age as beginning (or even ending) with the operettas. Some say it began with the little Princess musicals of Bolton, Wodehouse, and Kern (1915–1924) and their attempt to integrate story, character, and song. Others will say *Showboat* (1927) was the "first modern musical." *Oklahoma!* (1943) completed the integration of all the dramatic techniques by adding dance. For me, however, it begins with *On the Town* (1944), because dancers did not substitute for principals, because choreographer Jerome Robbins helped create the scenario, because his massive and fluid dance sequences carried the story in numerous places, and because he invented a brilliant new approach to musical comedy choreography: American theatre dance. It ends with *A Chorus Line* (1975), if not *Dreamgirls* (1981), because they were the last book musicals to be brilliantly staged. (Since then *Cats*, as an example, was impressively staged, what with having to tear out the roof of the Winter Garden just to get Grizabella up to the Heaviside layer, but its choreography is an ersatz combination of modern, tap, and ballet; nothing original, unique, or even stylish. One can only imagine what it would have looked like if Jerome Robbins or Bob Fosse had staged it.)

Nevertheless, I would not disagree with anyone who admires the entire twentieth century of staged musical entertainment.

Cast albums are recorded music. Scripts are literature. Concerts are readings. The recent proliferation of concert versions of musicals, from New York's *Encores!* to L.A.'s *Reprise!*, only serves to denude the American book musical of one half of its great achievement: staging. Even the other half, the scores, are better heard in their original recordings than in the recent complete or studio recordings in which they sing beautifully, but don't have enough rehearsal to project the full psychology of the role.

It's only on the stage, in full production, that the American book musical was a great work of art. To reproduce it accurately, or to create originals in a similar format, will require an understanding of a craft no longer regularly practiced, and nearly impossible to see in the flesh today: musical staging.

CHAPTER I

A Brief History

> *"The whole growth of our musical comedy can be seen through the growth of integration."*
> —Leonard Bernstein, *The Joy of Music*

For some historical perspective, let's first look briefly at a series of musicals, each of which brought something new to the form.

January 29, 1728: *The Beggar's Opera.* In London, England, author John Gay inserted 69 sets of lyrics into his original story of thieves in Soho, meant to be a satire on corruption in the upper classes but ultimately just a wonderful musical entertainment, variously cited as a "comic opera, "ballad opera," or "comical musical play." Notably, Gay wanted the songs done without accompaniment, so the actors could go *smoothly from scene to song and back again.* The producer overruled him, however, and various music, already popular, was applied. Revivals, revisions, imitations, and a flop sequel went on for 150 years, leading eventually to Gilbert and Sullivan.

September 12, 1866: *The Black Crook*. Various legends surround this production. This much is true: with a fire precluding the Academy of Music, two producers hustled their show over to Niblo's Gardens and opened this combination of French ballet and German melodrama, the first commercially successful combination of melodrama, song, dance, and spectacle. Thus the "first American musical" (a generally accepted moniker): a blend of song, dance, drama, and spectacle; a rising line of dramatic suspense, dances both solo and group, costumes both beautiful and erotic, stage machinery that exploits the setting, and popular music assigned to dramatic ideas. (Broken down to those elements, the American musical hasn't changed in 140 years!) This much is certain: musical extravaganzas were firmly established in America, and the outré costumes of the female ballet dancers caused a sensation and a run on the box office, particularly when local religionistas railed against the show. (The girls wore diaphanous skirts, through which the audience could see legs in tights.) The potpourri entertainment had a long run, and with revivals, tours, and imitators, entertained America for the next forty years. From this ancient artifact, let us add this much at least to our analysis of the American musical: (1) The combination of story and song may require a great leap of imagination—a willing suspension of disbelief—but when it works, it carries the story into our hearts with more emotion than any other work of art can. And (2) curtain raisers and afterpieces—entire farces and burlesques that played on the same bill with the feature production—were eliminated, and the entire evening (7:45 p.m. to 1:15 a.m. for *The Black Crook*) was devoted to a single drama. (The myth of *The Black Crook* as an accidental collaboration of an already existing, but bombing, melodrama at Niblo's and the stranded French girls was used as the plot in the 1954 Broadway musical *The Girl in Pink Tights*.)

July 27, 1874: *Evangeline*. First use of the description "musical comedy." (Possibly inaccurate, since it was really a burlesque—a spoof of a familiar story—of the Longfellow poem.) Also, the first entirely original musical score, written for the purpose by Edward E. Rice (music) and J. Cheever Goodwin (book and lyrics). Women playing men's roles, in pants, allowed for the display of female pulchritude. They were complemented by a male in drag as their top banana. (And by a dancing cow, who will continue down through the history of musicals to *Gypsy*.)

December 1, 1879: *H.M.S. Pinafore*. Pirated productions had been playing for over a year. This date marks the first official D'Oyly Carte production in America, and although American writers tried and tried, comic opera would be long forgotten if not for the Englishmen Gilbert and Sullivan. It is from W. S. Gilbert that all great American lyricists are descended, and with his comic operas, wit, as opposed to hokum, is introduced to America.

October 21, 1882. The Casino Theatre was built, the first specifically intentioned for musicals. Something was in the air.

September 4, 1884: *Adonis*. Long forgotten, and forgettable, it was carried by its star Henry E. Dixey, who seems to have been handsome, able to sing well and dance "adroitly," play comedy in a variety of guises, and willing to showcase his muscular thighs. Call *Adonis* the first "vehicle."

November 9, 1891: *A Trip to Chinatown* by Charles Hoyt. 650 performances make this the record holder of the nineteenth century. Two men and their girls pretend to take the title trip for cultural edification, but it's only a ploy to avoid a strict father. They're really going to a dance. A first for its American story and use of American pop songs such as "On the Bowery" and "After the Ball," *Trip* defines the early American musical: really an extended skit featuring familiar melodies with constant alterations, additions, and interpolations throughout its run.

April 4, 1898: *A Trip to Coontown.* Way off the mainstem, but nevertheless interesting, this is the first show produced, written, and performed by blacks (Bob Cole and Billy Johnson). White audiences were slow to attend, but . . .

July 5, 1898: The roof garden of the Casino now featured vaudeville, and when a short piece—*Clorindy, or The Origin of the Cake Walk*—joined the show, it was the first time a piece written and performed by black artists had left the minstrel circuit for a white theatre. The trend continued, and the creators (poet Paul Dunbar and composer Will Cook) eventually made it uptown with . . .

February 18, 1903: *In Dahomey.* The first full-length American musical written and performed by African-American talent in a Broadway theatre, and thus probably deserved of the title "the first black musical." It put the minstrel dance the Cakewalk on Broadway, which helped spark the coming dance craze. Though featuring the famous vaudeville team of (Bert) Williams and (George) Walker, it was far more successful when the producers took it to London, where it was exotic.

November 7, 1904: *Little Johnny Jones*. The American musical is born. ("Speed! Speed! And lots of it! That's the idea of the thing. Perpetual motion!"—George M. Cohan) Cohan had come from vaudeville, a medium in which you got on the audience's good side right away, or you were in physical danger. After two earlier attempts to conquer Broadway with expanded vaudeville skits, Cohan wrote the story of an American jockey in London, an ideal role for the pint-sized performer. Though filled with vaudeville shtick, it adhered to a strong plot line, featured outstanding tunes, and set up Cohan—who had written, directed, and starred in the production—as both a Yankee Doodle Dandy and the Man Who Owned Broadway. (The 1942 Warner Brothers film *Yankee Doodle Dandy*, starring James Cagney as Cohan, features a lengthy sequence from *Jones*.)

For the next three decades, Cohan's musicals, Ziegfeld's revues, and European operettas battled for Broadway audiences' attention with their very different kinds of stage musical entertainment. Musicals won, growing as they did less out of European influences than the American zeitgeist, and weathering both World War I, which soured even the Shuberts on German imports, and the Depression, which put an end to the extravagances of Ziegfeld.

1907–1931: *The Ziegfeld Follies*. Which isn't to say that Ziegy didn't leave behind one heck of a legacy. Sets and costumes (and star acts and beautiful, near-naked girls) will never not be a part of the American musical. Ziegfeld's talent was to present all four tastefully, though not, it seems, with the best of material. Very few of the songs written for his revues—which originally fielded a pamphlet of a plot, and quickly dispensed with even that—are well-remembered. Many of the stars, in fact, brought along their own material. Later this was frowned upon, when seasoned performers such as Bert Lahr, Zero Mostel, Pearl Bailey, Jerry Lewis, and Danny Kaye ad libbed their way through an author's plot, but it's still sometimes seen on Broadway, even in book musicals. Calling Nathan Lane.

December 8, 1914: *Watch Your Step*, "a syncopated musical show." An Irving Berlin revue, and his first full Broadway score. Berlin's ragtime songs introduced jazz to the theatre. The syncopated ragtime that would eventually define the music of America from Tin Pan Alley and the stages of Broadway, would triumph over the music of Europe, and would lead to the golden age of American theatre music. Irene and Vernon Castle introduced a plethora of syncopated dances in this "ragtime riot and dancing delirium," and for more than a decade, songs had to be danceable.

1915–1924: The Princess Theatre Musicals (*Nobody Home*; *Have a Heart*; *Very Good Eddie*; *Oh, Boy!*; *Leave It to Jane*; *Oh, Lady! Lady!!*; and *Sitting Pretty*). This series of musicals, often referred to as "gems," was created on a limited budget for a 299-seat theatre, encouraging its creators to write jokes that grew out of character and songs that grew out of plot, which Guy Bolton (book), P. G. Wodehouse (lyrics), and Jerome Kern (music) did with unusual wit and melody. Though not all were equally successful, this body of work defined the direction the book musical would go in. Make that American book musical, because in addition to their integrated approach, their stories were not set in Graustarkian principalities but American homes and gardens, and their characters were much closer to their audiences than the student princes of the operettas.

Wodehouse was the first lyricist since England's Gilbert to write literate and witty lyrics. Kern, though trained in European and classical music, began to write melodies and harmonies influenced by the rising sound of jazz and the dance craze. He introduced saxophones into the Broadway pit with his musical *Oh, I Say*. (Curiously, Kern fought the jazz craze in one unusual way. A strong-minded—some would say arrogant—man, he nixed any playing of his *Sitting Pretty* score outside of the theatre in different orchestrations. This only had the effect of keeping his songs a secret, and helped kill the show.) Another Kern innovation: "They Didn't Believe Me" (from an earlier Kern effort *The Girl From Utah*) and "Bill" (cut from *Oh, Lady! Lady!!* before it appeared in *Show Boat*) are considered the first "show ballads"—that is, songs in 4/4 time, where hitherto a score's ballads were in 3/4, or waltz, time. Bolton, Wodehouse, and Kern knew what they were doing, as evidenced by interviews they gave at the time in which they referred to their desire to integrate their work, rather than rely on the hodgepodge of comedians, random dances, and interpolated songs in the then-current formula for musical comedy.

May 23, 1921: *Shuffle Along*. Not the first (see *In Dahomey*), but the most successful black musical written and performed by African-Americans on Broadway. At the time it was pure entertainment. Today there'd have to be a vetting by the politically correct police. Unfortunately what is most notable is the absence of the black musical on Broadway for decades to come.

December 29, 1921: *Blossom Time*. An operetta, and thus something we would ordinarily pass over. (Not out of snobbery, mind you, simply because it remains a different, if unique, corner of stage musical entertainment.) But *Blossom* holds another patent. Adapted from the Viennese operetta *Das Dreimäderlhaus*, which had been an international success, the original began—and the Shubert's production established in America—the idea of setting lyrics to classical music, in this case using both the compositions and the life of Franz Schubert, arranged for Broadway by Sigmund Romberg, book and lyrics by Dorothy Donnelly. Although any number of famous classical composers were thereafter pillaged, the most notable that followed were: *Song of Norway* (1944)—lyrics by Robert Wright and George Forrest set to existing music by Edvard Grieg; the story a biography of the composer—*The Great Waltz* (1949)—Johann Strauss, also via Wright and Forrest; and finally, *Kismet* (1953)—wherein Wright and Forrest (didn't anybody else work in this genre?) used Alexander Borodin's music for a musical Arabian Night's tale based on a play of the same name.

September 2, 1924: *Rose-Marie*. Another operetta, but an interesting idea surfaces with Oscar Hammerstein II and Otto Harbach, authors of the book and lyrics. They refuse to have the song titles listed in the program. Their intention is to proclaim the integration of story and song!

December 1, 1924: *Lady, Be Good*. Brothers George and Ira Gershwin work together for the first time, and one of the greatest songwriting teams in American popular music is born. Though operettas were still very popular (*Rose-Marie* and *The Student Prince* were concurrent successes), the Gershwins solidified the introduction of American music with this twenties musical, featuring "Fascinating Rhythm" and "Little Jazz Bird." George Gershwin said he heard music in noise. The noise around him was America growing up.

Curiously, the simplistic *No, No, Nanette* and *Good News* were the most popular shows of the twenties, followed by the shows of Rodgers and Hart and the Gershwins, who were writing much more sophisticated songs than, say, "Tea for Two." Nevertheless, composers, beginning with Kern and Gershwin, began to push the boundaries of popular music, bringing a musical sophistication to Broadway scores that, little by little, gained acceptance.

October, 1927: On screen, *The Jazz Singer.* A Broadway play becomes the first "talkie," featuring several songs sung by Al Jolson. Song and dance would come quickly to cinema, forcing Broadway to begin to define itself more specifically, to offer the theatregoer what they couldn't get at the nickelodeon. The theatre would have to look to ideas and styles beyond the realism that film could offer.

December 27, 1927: *Show Boat.* Jerome Kern, who had written the Princess shows, and Oscar Hammerstein II, who had written many operettas, teamed up to take on the sprawling thirty-year story of three generations aboard a showboat, a very real form of floating theatre still plying the Mississippi at the time. At last the plot of a musical entertainment was taken as more than an unimportant, irrelevant device on which to hang songs, dances, and jokes. The book was American and serious, covering miscegenation, racism, alcoholism, and gambling. Mixed race lovers elope. There were no "bring on the girls" dance numbers. The score ranged from vaudeville ("Life Upon the Wicked Stage") to Negro spirituals ("Old Man River") to Blues ("Can't Help Lovin' That Man") to authentic ("After the Ball") to soaring, romantic operetta ("Why Do I Love You?"). Canonized as the greatest show of its time, it is considered to be first in either Americanizing the operetta or operettizing the American musical. Call it the first great American book musical. For our purposes, several things: listen to it for the melodies, harmonies, and rhythms that will become American theatre music. The story was the star, a shocking departure for the twenties. Watch the seventeen scenes flow by: engineering had come to stage craft. And know that Oscar Hammerstein II basically directed it. Although a bookwriter and lyricist, it is this man who will continue to develop an approach that will eventually culminate in the golden age of staging.

(And, credit where credit is due, Ziegfeld produced it. Remembered today only for his *Follies*, he was also a prolific producer of book musicals.)

October 29, 1929: The stock market crash. Not a musical. But the subsequent Depression, together with cheap admission to films, had an enormous effect on Broadway. Broadway responds with . . .

June 3, 1931: *The Band Wagon*. A financial and intellectual antidote to the spectacular revues of Ziegfeld. Small, smart, and sophisticated, material-oriented revues take over from the too-expensive-for-the-Depression lavish extravagances. Also, turntables may have been used for the first time in this production, a useful idea that increased the fluidity of Broadway staging enormously. And director-lighting designer Hazzard Short removed the footlights and hung lights from a rail on the balcony instead, giving light designers greater flexibility, and lighting a more natural look from then on. By the way, it starred Fred and Adele Astaire. Sister married English royalty and retired. Brother went on to become, due to the newly popular film musical, the first male American dance star.

Jumping backwards two years, we now have a story of one of the really unusual attempts to sophisticate the musical . . .

August 29, 1927: *Strike Up the Band*. George Kaufman wrote a savage anti-war satire, and George and Ira Gershwin wrote songs equally as incisive. Kaufman's biographer, Scott Meredith, explains:

> The usual practice in that period was to instruct the composer and lyricist merely to deliver a specified number of songs—a certain number of love songs, a certain number of dance songs—and then just fit them into the play at planned intervals whether or not the lyrics had anything much to do with the plot . . . Kaufman wanted . . . the music and lyrics to be integral to the play and its social point, either by furthering the plot development in the lyrics or by heightening and underlining the mood of the play . . . The brothers reacted with enthusiasm. They, too, worked harder than they had ever worked before, and every song they wrote, even the love songs, attempted to serve as emphasis for the savage and bitter attitudes of the play.

Although we have already seen Bolton, Wodehouse, and Kern strive to integrate their songs for the Princess Theatre musicals, their lighthearted plots needed only appropriate popular songs. The Gershwins were working on a more sophisticated story—anti-war—in a more sophisticated style—satire (which, Kaufman himself famously observed, is "what closes on Saturday night"). This one lasted two weeks in Philadelphia.

But producer Edgar Selwyn didn't give up. Although Kaufman didn't return to it, Morrie Ryskind rewrote the book, the Gershwins rewrote their score. And on . . .

January 14, 1930. The revised version opened on Broadway. Some historians believe the sharp edge was toned down for popular consumption, that theatregoers in the Coolidge era simply were not interested in the savage, raw, thought-provoking material. A closer look by Ethan Mordden (*Make Believe: The Musical Comedy in the 1920s*) claims the revised version wasn't much tamer, but that the first cast just wasn't famous enough. There were stars in those days. Or maybe that's just Philadelphia. (Having played there, I lean toward this last theory.) This time, on Broadway, it had a profitable run and successful tour. This success led the authors to write a second musical comedy satire . . .

December 26, 1931: *Of Thee I Sing*. Kaufman and Ryskind, with the Gershwins, lambast the American political system and the White House. The book is witty and satirical. The score is sophisticated, full of counterpoint, underscoring, recitative, and thematic writing. (If it wasn't so dedicated to the American vernacular, you'd swear it was comic opera.) It became the first ever musical libretto to win the Pulitzer Prize, and the first libretto to be published. Burns Mantle, complaining that the Pulitzer should go to a "play" and not a "musical," inadvertently gave it the perfect compliment for our discussion: "Strip it of its lyrics and its music and there will be little left of the prize winner but a half-hour of farcical and satirical sketches." Could there be a better definition of the truly integrated score?

November 21, 1934: *Anything Goes*. Score by Cole Porter, book by Guy Bolton and P. G. Wodehouse, and Howard Lindsay and Russel Crouse. Porter always rose to the occasion, and here his songs were (besides terrific, including many hits) beginning to see the efficiency of integration (a maturity he would complete with *Kiss Me, Kate*). Though not always evident in productions, the good old-fashioned *Anything Goes* is in fact a strong link between the musical comedy of the twenties and the modern musical, with its more flowing style and character-rich lyrics.

October 10, 1935: *Porgy and Bess*. Here's what you probably don't know: it wasn't very successful in its first incarnation. Thank goodness for subsequent productions, in which the original sniping of the music critics ("too Broadway") and theatre critics ("too opera") were subdued by the sheer audacity of the challenge and the heights to which George Gershwin's music soars. Gershwin did indeed desire to write "an American opera." American, serious, dialogue done as recitative in the purist versions, *Porgy* is a towering achievement that can scarcely be duplicated (though I'd venture that *Sweeney Todd* succeeds in much the same genre). But as far as pushing the American book musical along (and leaving aside the issue that its "book" is nearly all-sung), *Porgy* did wonderfully, as young composers surely must have taken note of the incredibly complex score, and young writers its serious, tragic story. An even more audacious musical for its time than *Show Boat*, the American musical form could forevermore serve up serious, significant dramas whenever its practitioners felt inspired. Note that its almost all-black cast was welcomed on Broadway, a race that had found so little work there previously that Gershwin had to beat the bushes for actors. (A proposed earlier version by other writers almost took place with Al Jolson in blackface.)

April 11, 1936: *On Your Toes*. Choreography by George Balanchine, he of the New York City Ballet, though not yet. Having been brought to America by Lincoln Kirstein to foster an American ballet company, Balanchine had any number of odd jobs until they were able to get under way. ("First a school, then a company."—George Balanchine) One of them was choreography for this musical by Rodgers and Hart and George Abbott. Initially a film for Fred Astaire, Hollywood never got that project off the ground, so Broadway saw hoofer Ray Bolger and prima ballerina Tamara Geva in the clever, if often confusing, story. What concerns us here, however, is the fact that three sequences were *written to be told in dance*, and Balanchine obliged. In Act One's "Princess Zenobia" ballet, Bolger, in the character of a vaudeville performer and music teacher, is shoved into a new ballet as a replacement for a corps de ballet member at the last minute, and hilariously bungles most of the steps. Act Two first features a showdown between ballet and tap dancers, and then climaxes in the famous "Slaughter on Tenth Avenue" ballet, in which Bolger begins dramatically dancing with the ballet star, but ends having to tap dance furiously while he dodges bullets from the star's gangster boyfriend. In short, it's only 1936, and plot is forwarded by dance.

January 13, 1940. This year's edition of *The Earl Carrol Vanities* marked the first use of microphones and amplification in Broadway theatres. The idea was lambasted by the critics, and discontinued.

December 25, 1940: *Pal Joey*. This Rodgers and Hart show caused consternation in the critical fraternity because the leading man is a gigolo, a bum, and a heel. Joey is a lowlife, willing to dally with an older, rich, married woman in order to have his own nightclub. She pays his rent for their den of iniquity, but he can't even remain monogamous for the money, and pretty much ends up back where he started. Joey, who is charming—he'd have to be—

is nevertheless selfish and ruthless, the American book musical's first anti-hero. Critic Brooks Atkinson famously wrote, "You can't draw sweet water from a sour well." But *Joey* proved you can, though it took a 1952 revival to confirm it. Also notable for the fact that the book writer, John O'Hara, was not from the theatre at all, but a famous author of short stories and novels. Because Gene Kelly starred in the original and Harold Lang in the revival, it became known as a dance musical, but it is something of a canard that *Pal Joey* blazed the way for *Oklahoma! Joey* features plenty of dance, but dance does not add to the plot or characters. Hollywood gave the role to a singing Sinatra without blinking. (And, heresy as this may be, it worked better.)

December 7, 1941. The Japanese bomb Pearl Harbor. America enters World War II, and quickly creates the greatest industrial base in history. Women come out of their homes, men go overseas, and everyone wants a respite from the war news. Two years later it arrives . . .

March 31, 1943. *Oklahoma!*'s success was overnight and enormous. It was what America wanted just when it wanted it, a collaboration of the lighthearted musical comedies of Rodgers and Hart and the sunny operettas of Hammerstein (with Kern, Romberg, and others), with just a dash of the darker side of life, from Lynn Riggs' play.

But for history we don't rely on commercial success. Here dance fully arrives, and in the first collaboration of the historic "Rodgers and Hammerstein." Rodgers had already had a long career with lyricist Lorenz Hart (dozens of shows, hundreds of songs) and Hammerstein had pursued a career in theatre from assistant stage manager on his uncle's shows to book and lyrics for *Show Boat*. It was, however, Agnes de Mille, the musical's choreographer, who made *Oklahoma!* into something more than a bucolic, melodic, sentimental, folk musical. Having spent years in vaudeville and ballet staging character- and story-driven dances, most recently the western ballet *Rodeo*, her "Dream Ballet" here stunned Broadway audiences for the psychological depth it brought to a dance number. (So much so that the director thought it gave away too much of the ensuing plot, and wanted it cut. Fortunately, and though theoretically he was right, other opinions prevailed.) No longer would the chorus girls come slipping out of the wings to every uptempo song, to perform a kick line, tap dance, or dance craze of the day. Henceforth dance would have to make a dramatic contribution. (Well, more than a few subsequent shows have trotted out the chorus for no reason other than waking up the audience. There's still musical *comedy*.) *Oklahoma!* was also the first "original Broadway cast album." Although various singers had recorded various songs from shows in the past, this was the first time the entire original cast recorded all their songs (on six 78 rpm's). Cast albums became very popular, and helped place theatre and theatre music at the apex of cultural life in America. In fact, the great popularity of the Broadway musical, fighting for attention with radio and film, and soon television, was kept alive by the invention of the cast album, at least for several more decades.

And one more thing. After trying for weeks to figure out an "opening number," Hammerstein and Rodgers gave up. No believable dramatic way to get the cowboys or chorus girls out there. So the show opened with an old woman churning butter, and a single cowboy singing a ballad. Offstage! A ballad! For the opening of a Broadway musical! He wanders on, singing. Chorus girls don't appear for another forty-five minutes, but the *story* is under way.

And so is the Rodgers and Hammerstein era. Romantic music, singing leads, and dancing or comedic supportive characters; believable story; and from now on, authors would try to make each element supportive of the basic story line and representative of time, place, and character.

For many years all shows had to have a dream ballet of some sort, and scene, song, and dance was thought best when equally balanced. Today, a stronger formula is: each to its necessary degree.

December 28, 1944: *On the Town.* Jerome Robbins and Leonard Bernstein (and designer Oliver Smith) became famous overnight when their one-act ballet *Fancy Free* debuted Robbins' character-based choreography and Bernstein's jazzy score for American Ballet Theatre. Shortly thereafter George Abbott was brought on board to direct, Comden and Green to write the book and lyrics. And the story of three sailors with only twenty-four hours leave in Manhattan and the desire to find a girl to share it with (great use of the ticking clock device) becomes a full-size Broadway musical. Although Bernstein's music was a revelation, both Jerome Kern (*Show Boat*) and George Gershwin (*Porgy and Bess*) had brought a serious composer's intricacies to Broadway before. What Bernstein did that was wholly original was write five—count 'em—five original suites of dance music for sequences to be illustrated by Robbins' choreography. Music for *Oklahoma!*'s "Dream Ballet" had been arranged by a "dance arranger" to the requirements of the choreographer, using the existing melodies of the songs in the show.

No one had yet created a composition specifically for a dance. And Robbins made a similar contribution. Whereas de Mille had taken a classical ballet vocabulary and worked it around to illustrate the cowboy characters ("turn in, not out!"), Robbins in his Broadway musicals began to work from the other direction. He would study the natural movements of his characters—with the city full of sailors this wouldn't have been difficult—and theatricalize that movement into dance steps. And thus was born the single most exciting part of the American book musical onstage: *American theatre dance*. In spite of the happy-go-lucky approach to their shore leave, and the sunny Comden and Green writing, Bernstein and Robbins brought a whole new level of sophistication and quality to musical comedy. Another milestone was Oliver Smith's set. While modernism and expressionism had swept through the world of art already, sets for musical comedies remained primarily realistic. Here Smith's Manhattan was done in light, airy, impressions. The set was art, not construction, a transition he would complete in the future for *West Side Story*.

April 19, 1945: *Carousel*. Having firmly established the most popular form of the current American musical with *Oklahoma!*, Rodgers and Hammerstein continued to propound it, adding nice touches here and there. One was the musical tragedy, for if poor Jud is dead at the end of *Oklahoma!*, he was after all only the villain. Here our (anti-) hero dies, leaving a wife and daughter. When he returns via a kindly angel to see his daughter graduate high school, there isn't a dry eye in the house, proving that an honest plot (Billy Bigelow's tragic flaw doomed him from the start) and strong emotion can trump a happy ending. Another was the soliloquy, the eleven o'clock inner monologue wherein the hero states his basic dilemma, here conveniently called "Soliloquy."

January 9, 1947: *Street Scene*. Not even a brief history of the American musical would be complete without a nod to composer Kurt Weill. Despite the fact that none of his Broadway shows were hugely successful (*Threepenny Opera* was written in Berlin before the Nazis chased him out), all of them boast wonderful scores, his music a cross between the commercialism of Broadway and the classicism he was trained for: *Lost in the Stars, Love Life, The Firebrand of Florence, One Touch of Venus, Lady in the Dark, Knickerbocker Holiday*, and *Johnny Johnson*. *Street Scene*, surely inspired by *Porgy and Bess*, has lasted the longest in opera repertoires. His shows almost always lacked focus and dramatic effect, as he too often worked with talented poets inexperienced with Broadway lyrics (Langston Hughes, Ogden Nash), books that barely held together, and directors and producers unable to contribute a confident and able hand. (Outside of a truly dazzling revival of one of his shows, which we may never see, he is best exemplified in his compilation revue *Berlin to Broadway with Kurt Weill*.)

October 10, 1947: *Allegro*. Rodgers and Hammerstein next turned away from big stories. Hammerstein fashioned an original book about a small town everyman, and the allegorical musical was born. Not without its dark side—the hero's wife is an adulteress—*Allegro* tells the story of Joe Taylor from birth to almost death. (Not coming full circle was a decision Hammerstein would later regret.) It featured formalistic staging, supporting characters, and the ensemble having most of the songs, which *commented upon* Joe's life. Didn't succeed, but the door to the "concept musical" was open.

December 30, 1948: *Kiss Me, Kate.* That Shakespeare could be musicalized was well-proven in Rodgers and Hart's earlier *The Boys From Syracuse* (1938). That it could be done so brilliantly in the modern American book musical form was established when Cole Porter, then a lion in winter, wrote some of his greatest songs for this Sam and Bella Spewack version of *The Taming of the Shrew,* in which a contemporary theatre company with a leading man and lady, divorced, are putting on a musical version of *The Taming of the Shrew.* Porter's score is remarkable for his ability to transition from the lighthearted songs that had made him famous to the substantial songs of the modern musical, without sacrificing his scintillating style and clever lyrics (and even more remarkable for coming at a time when most composers would be resting on their laurels, while Porter was resting on crutches, in constant pain). Thus the *Kate* score represents, besides Porter at the top of his talent, a great transition from the Rodgers and Hart songs to the Stephen Sondheim scores, with their lyrics adding to a character's profile and a show's themes with as much—in many cases more—sophistication as the dialogue. Though Sondheim cites Hammerstein as his mentor, I would have to argue that Porter's "Where Is the Life That Late I Led," with its clever rhymes *and* character delineation, is the template for songs such as "The Road You Didn't Take."

Some time after the opening of *Kate,* choreographer Hanya Holm notated her dances and registered them for copyright, the first time a choreographer had done so. Clearly choreographers were flexing their muscle, as their contributions were becoming increasingly important.

April 7, 1949: *South Pacific*. Continuing the formula they had established for the modern musical—the romanticism Rodgers wrote so well and the sentimentality Hammerstein limned with taste and subtlety—Rodgers and Hammerstein and Josh Logan (co-book and direction) created out of two short stories by James Michener one of the most powerful and entertaining Broadway musicals in history, alternately comic, romantic, and tragic. *South Pacific* is not listed here because of its sheer quality, however; Hammerstein solidified something that had been percolating around in his theatre-obsessed mind, probably for some time. Now he called it "continuous action." He had decided that the modern American musical should *flow*. No more blackouts, with the audience sitting in the dark as the stagehands changed the scenery and the orchestra replayed a tune. No more drops coming in just to cover a major scene change, with a supporting actor "in one" doing a song, dance, comic bit, or crossover. Eschewing a full stop anywhere outside intermission, Hammerstein wrote into this script a way in which each scene would flow into the next:

> (The lights fade out and a transparent curtain closes in on them. Before they are out of sight, the characters of the next scene have entered downstage in front of the curtain. All transitions from one scene to another in the play are achieved in this manner so that the effect is one of one picture dissolving into the next.)

This was a small step, nearly unnoticed and not remarked upon at the time, but it indicated the path that the great director-choreographers of the golden age would take to create the "cinematic flow" that became the ideal in musical theatre staging. (He wasn't the first, only the first in musical theatre, to suggest this. Harley Granville-Barker, the first modern British director, worked for a fluency in the staging of his own productions of Shakespeare, and argued for it in his writing: *Prefaces to Shakespeare, 1927–48.*)

November 24, 1950: *Guys and Dolls.* Frank Loesser (songs) and Abe Burrows (book) wrote a brilliant adaptation of the short stories by Damon Runyon, the great chronicler of the Broadway that is not so much Shubert Alley as Lindy's Deli, and the people not producers and actors but gamblers and night club habitués. But it was Michael Kidd's dances, from "Runyonland" to the "Crapshooter's Ballet," so stylized, so inimicable to the text, so representative of the characters in the same way that Runyon's famous prose was a stylized, comic representation of the real thing, that put *Guys and Dolls* on the map forever. (Curiously, director George S. Kaufman hated songs, and usually walked into the lobby when they were performed.)

March 29, 1951: *The King and I.* Rodgers and Hammerstein, still on a roll and having pioneered the tragic love story, came to "Anna and the King of Siam," an autobiographical book and subsequent play and film. Though Anna and the King can never be truly romantic, their relationship powers this classic story. What powers the score, however, is the Asian harmonies that make this if not the first Eastern-influenced theatre score, the first of the modern age. Rodgers score boasts both original melodies *and the ambience of the setting.* Nowhere more than in this exotic musical has the American musical showcased such a strong collaboration of the two ideas.

March 10, 1954: *Threepenny Opera.* The first Off-Broadway musical, and though its cast size has made it impractical for Off-Broadway ever since, it must be credited with starting that wonderful little theatre movement. Its long history is global. *The Beggar's Opera* had sparked Bertolt Brecht and Kurt Weill to write *Die Dreigroschenoper* in Berlin in 1928 on the same story. Translated into English as *The Threepenny Opera*, it earlier failed on Broadway but now proved a huge success off, and has been a staple of musical theatre the world over ever since. Although the Brecht/Weill style worked directly against Wagner's *gesamtkunstwerk*, insisting that the singers step out of the play to perform their songs, there's more than one way to stage this challenging musical.

March 11, 1954: *The Golden Apple.* Begun under the "rubric ballet/opera," serious composer Jerome Moross and literate lyricist John Latouche here set parts of Homer's *Iliad* and *Odyssey* in small-town Americana. Greatly favored by musical comedy fans for its ambitions (though never catching on with audiences), it is the first musical comedy to feature an all-singing, all-dancing approach, long before *Jesus Christ Superstar.*

May 13, 1954: *The Pajama Game.* New-to-Broadway Bob Fosse was recommended to George Abbott for Harold Prince's first producing credit. Also the first score by Adler and Ross. Fosse created "Steam Heat," as well as the picnic dance and the jealousy ballet, and thus modernized Robert Alton's line of show dancing with a style both character-driven and so dazzlingly theatrical and showstopping that he would henceforth be the style king.

October 20, 1954. *Peter Pan*, a theatre staple since James M. Barrie introduced it in London in 1902, becomes a musical for Mary Martin, and this successful version is canonized as *the* version. And

Cyril Ritchard will never not be Captain Hook. But the landmark here is subtle: Jerome Robbins solo directed and choreographed for the first time, and thus 1954 marks the advent of the auteur in musical theatre.

November 4, 1954: *Fanny*. Though only a pale imitation of the romantic Rodgers and Hammerstein formula (songs by Harold Rome when Rodgers refused to work with David Merrick), it marks Merrick's debut as a forceful and creative producer of musicals. He would become the most important and wide-ranging producer on Broadway for the next twenty-five years, always following the same formula: hire the most successful writers, directors, and stars, then bang their heads together.

May 5, 1955: *Damn Yankees*. The *Pajama Game* team reteamed. Producer Harold Prince told choreographer Bob Fosse he had sexy rising star Gwen Verdon, and told Gwen Verdon he had hot choreographer Bob Fosse. They met, and the greatest partnership since Lunt and Fontanne was born. This was the second score by newcomers Adler and Ross, but after the opening Ross died prematurely, and one can only imagine the jazzy theatre scores left unwritten.

Here's one for marketing. The advertisements featured Verdon in a baseball uniform. Weak box office. A few weeks into the run they put her into the famous bustier and sheer stockings now ubiquitous, and a stampede at the box office turned the show into a hit.

March 15, 1956: *My Fair Lady*. Alan Jay Lerner and Frederick Loewe certainly knew that Rex Harrison couldn't sing, as well as they knew that Profession Henry Higgins, George Bernard Shaw's great creation, might be out of character if he did. No problem. Besides the fact that Julie Andrews could do the heavy lifting, Loewe had been born in Berlin in 1904, his father a light comedian in operetta. There a "talk-song" style evolved in which actors, not singers, essayed the songs. He would have been familiar with *singspiel*, a German form in which the spoken word was of primary importance in a few songs within a light drama, and *sprechgesang* ("speech song") or *sprechstimme* ("speech voice"). The idea evolved directly through operetta in Europe to comic opera (Gilbert and Sullivan) in England. And so it came to pass that Professor Higgins would have his patter songs, and the American book musical could, from then on, feature a character who could sing without booming out high notes.

Besides becoming the Broadway score against which all others are judged, *My Fair Lady*, with the sequence in which Eliza learns to talk like a lady, introduced the montage, already popular on screen but new to the stage.

According to Lerner, in 1952, when he and Loewe first struggled with the idea of *Pygmalion* as a musical, they gave up, because the play did not contain the requisite secondary subplot—usually another love story for the dancers (*Kiss Me Kate*) or the comics (*Guys and Dolls*), though sometimes for more singers (*South Pacific*)—nor any opportunity for chorus boys and girls to strut their stuff, nor a happy ending. By 1954, however, when they returned to the project, the American musical had indicated broader opportunities of form. Perhaps it had, with productions in the early fifties of *The King and I*, *A Tree Grows in Brooklyn*, *Threepenny Opera*, and *The Golden Apple* appearing—all musicals that didn't adhere closely to a known formula. Nevertheless, one has to credit Lerner and Loewe themselves with creating musical sequences for *My Fair Lady* only out of the ideas "already in the text," (Lerner) and not forcing in numbers outside the drama in order to satisfy the still-current musical comedy formula. This idea (surfacing as early as 1943, when Hammerstein, after much angst, decided to let *Oklahoma!* begin with a woman churning butter) completed the revolution of the American musical theatre to an entirely story-driven art form.

May 3, 1956: *The Most Happy Fella*. Frank Loesser had already provided us with *Where's Charley?* and *Guys and Dolls*, both in firmly musical comedy forms, so there was little warning that his next musical would be so ambitious. *Fella* is musical comedy, but with plenty of ambition thrown in. And it satisfied. With thirty songs and orchestrations for a large orchestra, and three acts long (very, in some productions), it might be called musical comedy *extremis* but for its story, which is romantic/tragic. (Older man woos younger woman in letters, sends a photo of a younger man. Nevertheless, love grows between woman and older man, but at the crucial moment she finds herself pregnant by younger man.) Still, there's enough comedy (Boys: "Standing on the Corner" and Waitress: "Ooh! My Feet!"), and romantic duets ("My Heart Is So Full of You") for all tastes. If the final result didn't really break any new ground, it's listed here for its ambition and audacity, a direct link between *Show Boat* and *Porgy and Bess* of the earlier age, and *West Side Story* and *Sweeney Todd* shortly to come.

September 26, 1957: *West Side Story*. Book by Arthur Laurents; music by Leonard Bernstein; lyrics by Stephen Sondheim; conceived, directed, and choreographed by Jerome Robbins. Hard upon all the achievements of the past, and in an era when producers were trying to produce good shows and hoping they would be successful—as opposed to latterly, when producers are trying to produce successful shows, and hoping they'll be good—Robbins, Bernstein, and Laurents decided to write a modern *Romeo and Juliet*. That the plot had plenty of room for song and dance was a no-brainer, since ballet and opera versions of Shakespeare's original had already proved practical. Robbins, with one foot in musical comedy, the other in ballet, had every intention to tell whole sections of the story with pure dance. What makes *West Side Story* a textbook musical is that these sequences are performed by the actors who play the roles. No Dream Curly here. Robbins cast about for young men and women who could sing *and* dance *and* act. (None of the adult roles sing or dance, a conceit that gives the "generation gap" theme a subtle push.) The "continuous action" of Hammerstein reached its peak as Robbins created scene after scene that flowed freely and seamlessly through dialogue, song, and dance, and from sequence to sequence. Even if Bernstein's very sophisticated music took a few years and a film version to catch on, everyone can whistle it today.

While the first great revolution in musical theatre had been the embracing of realism (begun by the efforts of the Princess Musical authors to keep their stories contemporary and American) and to have their jokes and lyrics grow out of character, the musical as proposed by Bernstein and Robbins (and, in particular, the settings of Oliver Smith) here for the first time embraced impressionism. A look at the poster/window card for the original production, especially compared to previous advertisements for musicals, hints at the lyricism behind every aspect of the production. Even the dialogue was intended by Laurents to be in short, swift segments. Without giving up truth in character, acting, and story, *West Side Story* added a production style that lifted the American musical out of the scenic heavy, naturalistic extravaganza it had become bogged down in.

Far from pointing the way to a new, singular, lyric style in musicals, what *West Side Story* ended up doing was pointing out that any style could be appropriate, provided it was generated from, and supportive of, the text.

With the success of *West Side Story*, the American musical had completed its evolution, and become an amalgam of the popular forms of entertainment (minstrel shows, vaudeville, extravaganza, spectacle, burlesque) and the more intellectual forms of theatre (drama, opera, ballet), losing sight of neither the commercial aspects of the former nor the classical aspirations of the latter.

December 19, 1957: *The Music Man.* Less than two years after Henry Higgins captivated audiences without holding a note for more than a nanosecond, Meredith Wilson gave the same technique to Harold Hill. What better approach for a con man to con than through the now established patter song technique? Robert Preston was brilliant at it, warning the small-town chorus about the new downtown attraction ("Trouble in River City") and then offering them a solution ("76 Trombones"). Even the chorus got into the act ("You Gotta Know the Territory"). Once again the female lead had the melodies (Barbara Cook). Midwest Americana and small town sentiment carried this musical to classic status, but it's the patter songs that make it unique.

February 5, 1959: *Redhead*. Having married his muse, Bob Fosse stepped up to directing. (Gwen Verdon and the title was surely a hot ticket, but no, it is the killer in this murder mystery musical whose hair and beard are red.) By now de Mille and Robbins had integrated the dance sequence, and dance was an equal partner in storytelling. Fosse, however, here created the *dance show*. Built on an idea that never delivered much of a script, Fosse demanded a big empty stage, used most of the time for his star and his dance corps, with set pieces coming and going at his whim, and dazzled critics and audiences with dance number after dance number. After dance number after dance number. Some of them didn't even require lyrics. He created the *vaudeville musical* as well, a form few others ever utilized, but which became his trademark. From *Redhead* to *Sweet Charity* to *Pippin* to *Chicago*, Fosse's style was presentational. Watch this! And this! Storytelling as minor adjunct to song and dance. Funny—just when the Rodgers and Hammerstein formula had made the musical comedy into the musical play, here's an auteur director-choreographer serving entertainment over story and wowing audiences.

May 21, 1959: *Gypsy*. Jule Styne (music), Stephen Sondheim (lyrics), and Arthur Laurents (book) wrote the quintessential showbiz musical for Ethel Merman when David Merrick optioned the autobiography of stripper Gypsy Rose Lee. Michael Bennett once defined the difference between a "hot" musical and a "cold" musical by its setting, pointing out that when the story involves performers, they can perform. They can deliver their songs flat out to the audience and, if they're good enough, knock 'em dead, always useful to the success of a musical comedy; whereas a book number has to be sung in context, the famous fourth wall in theatre carefully observed. (Thus so many showbiz stories in film musicals, where realism is an even higher barrier.) Bennett was being a little disingenuous, because while *Follies* could feature hot numbers and *Company* could not, he nevertheless managed to stop *Company* several times with some of the best showbiz staging ever. Nevertheless, if there's nothing like a show business story—and nothing like the *Lear*-like mom in *Gypsy*—it's "Let Me Entertain You" in all its forms, from vaudeville to burlesque; "All I Need Is the Girl," in which a supporting character shows off his new act; and "You Gotta Have a Gimmick," in which strippers strut their stuff (one of the funniest and most raucous numbers in all of musical theatre), that carry this musical between Merman's moments. And if the hot musical was done before—perhaps *Show Boat* was the first major use of a showbiz milieu—nobody did it better than Robbins' staging of Jule Styne's brassiest score. Right up to the finale, when Mama Rose struts her sad stuff on the runway, this is the hottest of the hot musicals, without sacrificing one goose bump of the drama.

April 14, 1960: *Bye Bye Birdie*. Although firmly in the musical comedy genre, *Birdie* peeked in at rock and roll and found it welcoming. Conrad Birdie (né Elvis Presley) sang and gyrated to the pulsating rhythms then pushing into American entertainment ("Honestly Sincere"). Others pulsed to jazz ("A Lot of Livin' to Do"). Rounded out with great humor—the Handel-esque "Hymn for a Sunday Evening," the cantorial "Normal American Boy," the tango "Spanish Rose"—the score launched the careers of the supremely melodic and wonderfully rhythmic Charles Strouse and the splendidly comedic Lee Adams. But oh what they foreshadowed with those rock 'n roll chords of "One Last Kiss."

May 3, 1960: *The Fantasticks*. Never really duplicated, and forming no link in the history of the American book musical, this Tom Jones and Harvey Schmidt Off-Broadway concoction nevertheless features the greatest example of substance over spectacle ever mounted in a theatre. Hundreds of small Off-Broadway musicals have come and gone since, yet none have captured the combination of theatricality, rich musicality, and poetic innocence of this one. Most have either been spoofs or revues with threadbare excuses for a book. This little musical stands alone, with one of the strongest scores ever written for a book musical, the songs never better performed than with just the harp and piano of the original production. One of Off-Broadway's very few great American book musicals.

September 29, 1960: *Irma La Douce*. The little French musical that could. With almost no scenery, a cast of one woman and sixteen men, a narrator, French chansons in the Edith Piaf mold (translated), touches of vaudeville and burlesque, and settled in the smallish 1,000 seat Plymouth Theatre, this story of a poule and her mec (a whore and her pimp!) that even Walter Kerr didn't find dirty was a great success, demonstrating that, even on Broadway, small, smart, and funny could work also.

October 14, 1961: *How to Succeed in Business Without Really Trying*. Fosse hit his stride with this show, in spite of what you've heard about "Steam Heat" in *Pajama Game* and his teaming up with Gwen Verdon for the first time in *Damn Yankees*. Less pure dance, but Fosse's staging of Frank Loesser's hysterical songs—along with

Michael Kidd's *Guys and Dolls* choreography—gave American theatre dance the highly stylized look—cartoons come to life—that dazzled audiences worldwide for years to come.

May 8, 1962: *A Funny Thing Happened on the Way to the Forum.* Burt Shevelove and Larry Gelbart introduced Sondheim to the raucous Roman comedies of Plautus, and this burlesque/farce musical was born. It's the musical comedy in which the songs are musical relief from the breakneck comedy. Only Sondheim (or Cole Porter before him) could possibly create songs so clever by themselves that it doesn't matter that they don't advance the plot or delineate character—an interesting idiom, but one to be wary of.

October 3, 1962: *Stop the World I Want to Get Off* and
May 16, 1965: *The Roar of the Greasepaint, the Smell of the Crowd.* Both English imports to Broadway starring Anthony Newley. *Stop the World* is set in a circus arena, wherein an everyman's life is played out, and *Greasepaint* on a game board, wherein the haves and have-nots play against each other, with the haves changing the rules to suit themselves. Though *Greasepaint* didn't last long, "Who Can I Turn To?" became one of the most recorded songs of all time. *Stop the World* is firmly in the allegory mode, due to its birth-to-death story, metaphoric style, unit set, Greek chorus, and *Hamlet*-sized leading male role. Perhaps because they are English (a production starring Sammy Davis Jr. was one of the worst-staged revivals in history) they are fairly obscure. Both are early concept musicals and allegory musicals, successful where *Allegro* was not.

January 6, 1963: *Oliver!* also came from England. This show and the two imports above are the first, and until Andrew Lloyd Webber, the only, English musicals to impress the American theatregoer. *Oliver!*'s great contribution, however, is very American. The double turntable set of Sean Kenny allowed this musical—one with no dancing—to flow smoothly and look great. Also, all three shows disregarded the traditional drops-and-wagons set design and went environmental, a huge new addition to a designer's options.

January 16, 1964: *Hello, Dolly!* When Gower Champion staged this Jerry Herman score and Michael Stewart book, the light comedy it was based on—Thornton Wilder's *The Matchmaker*—wasn't on his mind. Topping himself was. He'd dazzled audiences with *Bye Bye Birdie*'s cacophonous "Telephone Hour," and opened *Carnival* by building a carnival right before our eyes. He opened *Dolly!* with a street scene, had two dozen apprentices dancing in Horace Vandergelder's feed store, climaxed the first act with a parade, opened the second with a multitude of waiters racing here and there in choreographed chaos, and surrounded Dolly Levi with dozens of men for what could have been an interminable (but was instead showstopping,) title song. (In the early stages of development, David Merrick invited Hal Prince to direct. Prince declined, in a letter that went on to say something like, "whatever you do, cut the title song. Dolly is not a woman who would ever go to a fancy restaurant." When the show opened, Prince wanted the letter returned, but Merrick preferred to hang it on his office wall.) The staging was well-integrated, but it was also *the point*. It was musical staging—Busby Berkeley staging—as spectacle, and Broadway really hadn't seen anything like it since the days of casts of hundreds. But those hussars generally just stood around and strained their top notes. The sweep and Swiss-clock–like coordination of the chorus numbers—Champion used a runway that circled the orchestra pit—swept audiences to their feet. It was as if the ambitious director-choreographer was saying, "Top this." And for sheer scope and staging-as-spectacle, no one ever has.

March 26, 1964: *Funny Girl*. Stars have always been a part of the American musical, and when little-known Barbra Streisand played Fanny Brice, she fully arrived. Unlike *Dolly* and *Fiddler*, this vehicle requires someone just that good, partly because the character *is* a star, and partly because, due to the subsequent, well-made film, Streisand's performance has been canonized. Although theatre scores were slowly being edged out by rock (1964 featured several Beatles hits and Louis Armstrong's recording of "Hello, Dolly!" at the top of the charts), Jule Styne's "People" hit the popular consciousness (even if "Don't Rain on My Parade" and "The Music That Makes Me Dance" are superior songs). But there had been vehicle musicals for years. The landmark here is a smaller but significant one. Streisand's voice, born to be recorded but not for the stage, came to us via the first personal wireless microphone (hidden in her costume, and given during tryouts to broadcasting local police calls). Today everyone onstage looks like a telephone operator, and we're supposed to ignore that fashion accessory.

September 22, 1964: (What a year!) *Fiddler on the Roof*. Jews go to the theatre, everyone knew that. Sholom Aleichem was already a respected teller of tales of the shtetel. But no one knew that such humanity could be contained in a musical. Uber-director-choreographer Jerome Robbins staged it, and Jerry Bock's music,

Sheldon Harnick's lyrics, and Joseph Stein's book (and the Boris Aronson sets in the Chagall style) so captured the tragedy of the poor, pious, and tradition-bound Jewish community inside the anti-Semitic Russian monolith that audiences wept. Yes, wept.

Dolly! and *Fiddler* would battle it out for years, ending as the two longest-running Broadway musicals of their day, proving that when staged well, both musical comedy and musical drama could bring in the crowds. (Or were these long runs a battle of producer egos between the last two great impresarios?)

November 22, 1965: *Man of La Mancha*. Edna Ferber gave Hammerstein and Kern the stage rights to her novel *Show Boat* believing it couldn't be a musical. *Porgy and Bess* lost money. Out of town, *Oklahoma!* caused this to appear in Walter Winchell's column: "No girls, no jokes, no chance." Some of the greatest names in Broadway songwriting had turned down the chance to turn Shaw's *Pygmalion* into a musical, claiming that it couldn't be done. *West Side Story*'s first producer gave up—she couldn't raise the money; the ballet/opera was thought to be an overindulgence of its creators.

And in 1889 an operetta version of Cervantes Spanish novel *Don Quixote de La Mancha* by Reginald De Koven and Harry B. Smith failed on Broadway. "I doubt that a successful play, musical or otherwise, can be made of Don Quixote," Smith said on reflection.

So much for the naysayers of Shubert Alley.

Man of La Mancha could only find a naive, neophyte producer, could only raise about half the money usual for a Broadway musical of the period, couldn't get a regular theatre— instead talked one that was about to be torn down into staying open for one more show—and then, finally, became one of the most beloved musicals of all time. But its philosophy ("To Dream the Impossible Dream") and its tuneful flamenco-based score that drove it to success, aren't what concerns us here. Two things: it utilized a single set. Howard Bay had designed a stark, gloomy dungeon, its only access a steep, towering staircase. Within this prison, a few rough-hewn tables and chairs were moved around, but most was left to our imagination. And it was, certainly relatively speaking, a very stark drama for a 1965 musical. Don Quixote was an eccentric dreamer, blind to the fun others couldn't resist making of him, who died in the end. Aldonza was raped in front of our eyes. Between *Fiddler* and *La Mancha*, it is surely true that no one thinks a serious story can't be musicalized any longer. Except, of course, producers. By now virtually any and all material could be adaptable to the musical stage. The horizons of the American book musical are limitless.

January 29, 1966: *Sweet Charity*. Bob Fosse was well-established as both a choreographer and director (*Pajama Game, Damn Yankees, Bells Are Ringing, New Girl in Town, Redhead, How to Succeed, Little Me*). Gwen Verdon was well-established as a star dancer (*Alive and Kicking, Can-Can, Damn Yankees, New Girl in Town, Redhead*). They were well-established as a team, and married. *Charity* doesn't offer much in the way of new or landmark moments/ ideas, just a brilliant dance show with a very funny book by Neil Simon. But because Fosse conceived the idea (from an Italian film) and wrote the first draft, it deserves a place in the developing line of auteur-director musicals. Also, there hadn't been a star female dancer since Ziegfeld's Marilyn Miller. And it is the best musical of Dorothy Fields—the first lady lyricist of Broadway.

November 20, 1966: *Cabaret*. There's a great deal of talk about the concept musical, pioneered by this one. Just what a concept musical is has never quite been clear, except that it comes from the fertile mind of producer-director Harold Prince, by way of *Allegro*, and when it works—*Cabaret, Company, Follies*—it's great, and when it doesn't—*Sweeney Todd, Pacific Overtures*—it undercuts the material. (Okay, that last is opinion. More later.) Though many milieus had been staged, Nazi Germany hadn't been one of the most popular. And although the show-within-the-show was an old trope, the cabaret numbers here limn the book action brilliantly, thus the "comment" song. Decadence was glitzed, while the ugliness of anti-Semitism wasn't softened. Book numbers and onstage numbers alternated smoothly, and the stylized choreography of Ron Field—a talented comet who flamed out too early in the theatrical firmament—captured the frenzy of the Weimar Republic. Kander and Ebb arrived as well, with those belt-'em-out songs that energize performers and audiences alike.

November 12, 1967. Producer David Merrick recast his long-running success *Hello, Dolly!* with Pearl Bailey, Cab Calloway, and an all-black cast, thereby re-energizing the idea of the black musical, which had been dormant since the 1920s. The production was sensational, sizzling, and scintillating. There followed any number of feeble attempts to cash in on the same idea, with a rewritten *Kismet* as *Timbuktu!* (1978) featuring Eartha Kitt, and a *Guys and Dolls* (1977) featuring television's Robert Guillaume and a disco-ized score. (For which the Actor's Equity announcement read: "Auditions for the all-black production of *Guys and Dolls*," gave the time and place, and then read, "All calls will be conducted without regard to race, creed, color, or religion.") Though both black versions were dreadful, Broadway was waking up to the plethora of black talent waiting in the wings.

January 13, 1968: *Your Own Thing* (Off-Broadway) and April 29, 1968: *Hair*. The sixties begin. And bring the downfall of the American book musical score. Way back in 1952, rock and roll was introduced to American audiences as a new musical form. (Developed, curiously enough, out of the same minstrel music, ragtime, jazz, and rhythm and blues from which Tin Pan Alley and theatre music had evolved.) Recently both the Beatles and Dean Martin could sell records. But the Italian crooner's day was dusking, and popular music would henceforth be rock and roll–based. While Broadway musicals had for almost a century boasted the most popular music in the country, theatre music would, very gradually, be edged out of the limelight, out of the front record bins, into a marginalized world so small that what had once sold millions of records (*My Fair Lady, Cabaret*) would one day not be worth recording commercially. (As recently as 1956, Columbia Records found it profitable to put up the entire investment for *My Fair Lady* in exchange for recording rights.) *Hair*'s infectious light-rock/pop melodies combined with hip, modern, and in many cases filthy lyrics, captured the public. The show itself was staged in a wildly theatrical, avant-garde style by Off-Broadway's reigning king of grunge, masks, props, and anti-slick staging, Tom O'Horgan. That particular style, ideal for the anti-war, anti-establishment themes of *Hair*, would not be particularly useful for other musicals. But its rock music would. The writing was on the wall. Jesus Christ himself was coming to rock you.

December 1, 1968: *Promises, Promises.* Remember the microphones critics hated in *Earl Carroll's Vanities?* They're back, and this time, accustomed to studio recordings on LPs and radio, no one objected when an entire sound system invaded Broadway. With a score by Bachrach and David, writers already hugely successful in the recording field, this slick musical augmented its onstage singers with voices in the pit, miked everyone, and employed a sound engineer to sit in the back of the theatre and carefully balance all the music and singing. If members of the audience in the balcony heard the show coming from speakers to the side of the theatre rather than the lips of the cast, they didn't seem to complain too much. Henceforth, all Broadway musicals would have to employ sophisticated sound systems. While *Promises'* songs fit smoothly into the urban story, they are, fundamentally, pop- and not theatre-based. Additionally, the musical was chock-full of experienced professionals, and one young choreographer staged the musical numbers in such a way as to herald, particularly in "Grapes of Roth," a new integration in staging: Michael Bennett.

Coming soon: popmeister Lloyd Webber and the erudite and sophisticated Sondheim battle it out for decades over the form of American musical entertainment. Sondheim fires the first volley.

April 26, 1970: *Company.* In addition to its use of the comment song from the ensemble, which Hammerstein had begun in *Allegro,* this George Furth (book), Stephen Sondheim (music and lyrics), Hal Prince (direction), and Michael Bennett (musical staging) musical dispensed with a chorus. And a plot. The fourteen principals became the ensemble. The book, which had evolved from a series of short playlets on the subject of relationships, was not a story but variations on a theme. The central bachelor character was used simply as a connection to illustrate the *mishegoss* of five couples and three girlfriends. Further, this chorus-less musical was the most interestingly staged in years. Without chorus girls, Bennett succeeded in stopping the show (with "Company," "Side by Side by Side," "You Could Drive a Person Crazy," and "Tick Tock,") while keeping both the flow and the ideas moving forward. The non-linear musical fully arrived a year later with the historic musical . . .

April 4, 1971: *Follies*, when Stephen Sondheim, Hal Prince, and Michael Bennett regrouped around a James Goldman backstage story. "Everything is possible," reads a Sondheim lyric from the show and the title of the published chronicle of the making of *Follies* by its production assistant. Indeed it must have been, for never had a musical taken on such an unusual form, and an unusual theme. Although dark stories had long been a part of the American musical, going all the way back to *Show Boat, Pal Joey,* and *Carousel,* this one tops the list: at a reunion of *Follies* girls, four adults survey the wreckage of their lives. Again no story, just variations on a theme. Sondheim's songs successfully reached an apex of ambition, divided between book songs that illuminated their characters, "pastiche" songs in the style of the revue composers of the original period that also illustrated character, and showstopping numbers (again, brilliantly staged by Bennett, now sharing director billing as well) in classical musical comedy style. From the ghost of a *Follies* show girl that begins the eerie prologue to the emotional collapse of the leading man as he performs in an imaginary *Follies,* we are rendered (in exquisite sets and costumes that could not be duplicated today for either money or talent) the intimate and searing emotional power of the wrong choices, calculated choices, and pragmatic choices of our lives. In a stunning change of form that even critics hadn't yet caught on to, it was with Sondheim that the lyrics more than the dialogue came to plumb the depth of each character, and etch the strongest themes of the story. Because Sondheim's lyrics are dialogue, Goldman and future librettists working with him would have less and less to do.

October 12, 1971: *Jesus Christ Superstar.* Lloyd Webber fires back, and the poperetta is born. Written and first produced as a record, *Superstar* has become a worldwide hit of the musical stage, primarily for its score, which is all there is; no dialogue included. If *Golden Apple* had introduced the all-singing, all-dancing musical, *Superstar* now introduced the singing-only musical, dispensing even with dance. But what it really dispensed with would eventually change the American musical forever. *The music bore no relationship to the setting.* Theatre music was replaced with popular music, now not only in the record bins, but in the theatre as well. A production of *Superstar* is always something of a dramatic conundrum. Either the show is costumed in the glitzy, glam rock style of the original Broadway production, in which case the characters—Jesus and Mary et al.—are wildly out of place, or the costumes—as has been the case in most productions since—are the robes and sandals of the period, in which case the music is wildly out of period. The would-be *Superstar* director's greatest challenge—which concept?— hasn't slowed the musical's popularity. It has, however, ended, at least in large swaths of the musical theatre business, the notion that all the pieces would combine to support the drama, to create a synergy that delivered the story to the audience without detour. This new conundrum has paralyzed composers of the American book musical, who feel old-fashioned and uncommercial if they write with an ethnic, regional, or period flavor indigenous to their story, yet cannot find enough contemporary stories of interest to justify the latest in pop music. Call it the beginning of the end of the golden age.

October 20, 1971: *Ain't Supposed to Die a Natural Death* ("Tunes From Blackness") and May 16, 1972: *Don't Play Us Cheap!* Each ran less than a season, and are seldom mentioned in musical comedy compendiums. Both were collections of rap songs by Melvin Van Peebles. The first was primarily revue; the second had a bit of a story. The author wanted his words spoken more than sung so that audiences could understand them! Note the dates. Rap itself was just developing in the Bronx; the first rap record didn't arrive for eight more years (though both these shows were recorded). Most critics find *Porgy and Bess* to be a white version of black life, wherein the inhabitants of Catfish Row are happy with plenty of nuthin'. Here authentic black characters in Harlem "said" many authentic things in a fresh and powerful fashion about real black life.

October 23, 1972: *Pippin*. Bob Fosse took a tuneful pop score from the fresh and lyrically clever pen of Stephen *"Godspell"* Schwartz that, with book by Roger Hirson, told the story of the son of King Charlemagne, and staged an epic opus of flesh and showbiz sassiness. Though it angered the composer, it was certainly Fosse's slick staging, complete with the wildly energetic Leading Player (Ben Vereen becomes a star) and a singalong conducted by *The Beverly*

Hillbillies' venerable Irene Ryan, that instigated the long run. Fosse having already risen to choreographic heights with *Sweet Charity*, it isn't the staging that places *Pippin* on this list. Shortly after it opened, Fosse directed a television commercial for the show, the first, and still one of the most creative, in theatre history. If it broadened Broadway's audience base, it also raised the cost of producing a Broadway musical, as TV time is expensive. (Years before, *Camelot* had turned from a show that was closing after a few months to a resounding success, based on an appearance by its principals, Julie Andrews, Richard Burton, and Robert Goulet, singing a good many of its songs on *The Ed Sullivan Show*.)

February 25, 1973: *A Little Night Music*. Going his lonely way, Stephen Sondheim actually took a step back from both the pastiche of a *Follies* milieu and the zetz of urban New York to adapt an Ingmar Bergman film (*Smiles of a Summer Night*) that takes place at the turn of the century (not this one, the old one) and called for an operetta-like (if ebulliently sexy) score, all in variations of 3/4 time. He wanted to score all of it, but Prince, afraid of the "opera" connotation with fickle Broadway audiences (and wisely realizing that if you sing everything, the power of individual songs is reduced), brought in librettist Hugh Wheeler for some dialogue. Like *Follies*, that dialogue serves merely as music-relief and transitional material. The real depth of the piece, the emotional lives of the characters and the story's significance, are all in the songs, particularly the lyrics, of which by now, Sondheim was acknowledged as the reigning master in the literate tradition of Wodehouse and Gilbert. *Night Music* is in fact a glorious updating of the comic opera form (its title even a translation of Mozart's *Eine Kleine Nachtmusik*).

October 18, 1973: *Raisin* won the Tony Award over *Candide*, *Seesaw*, and *Gigi*, yet is seldom spoken of in the same context today. *Raisin*'s score doesn't rise to the commercial level of any of its then-competitors, yet is nicely jazz-based and supportive of the text. What concerns us, however, is that, for nearly the first time ever, a black musical about African-American characters and their travails was in fact based on the powerful, award-winning, and still studied play *A Raisin in the Sun* by Lorraine Hansberry. *In Dahomey* and *Shuffle Along* were really minstrel shows dressed for uptown, and Pearl Bailey's *Hello, Dolly!* was a black version of a white musical. Here we have a musical drama presenting the black experience. With the two exceptions of the Melvin Van Peebles rap shows, that hadn't happened before, and (*Dreamgirls* aside) hasn't happened often enough since.

June 3, 1975: *Chicago*. What was to be the apex of the dual careers of Gwen Verdon and Bob Fosse became a musical laden with problems. First was the heart attack of its director (subsequently referenced in his film *All That Jazz*), postponing rehearsals for nine months. Then came the backstage bickering, with Verdon defending Fosse's dictatorial approach (in his next two shows, *Dancin'* and *Big Deal*, he dispensed with living authors) and lyricist Fred Ebb and Fosse collaborating on a libretto that might have done better in the hands of a third party. And finally there was the darkness of the material, which approached *Follies* for its cynicism. This in an era that would soon provide the spirit-lifting *A Chorus Line* and the sunny *Annie*. Vaudeville, however, was the really original notion here. Subtitled "the vaudeville musical," most of the songs in *Chicago* were staged as "in one" numbers directly to the audience. Most explained or commented on the action. But it came at us too often in a tight, dark, minimalist style. Its failure to bloom with the public, however, may also have been because, one month later, audiences were rocked by a tsunami of a new musical that buried the history of *Chicago* for twenty years, until a successful revival and film version would deliver a wittier book and music video–style staging and editing to a more cynical culture that gave the musical far more notoriety than it developed initially.

July 25, 1975: A Chorus Line. Integration reaches its zenith, partly because the material, shaped by composer Marvin Hamlisch, lyricist Edward Kleban, book writers James Kirkwood and Nicholas Dante (and even Neil Simon for a few good jokes), came from long, thoughtful, real-life interviews of real dancers. In a gradual winnowing of material and improvisations over more than a year, these became the book. Another reason for its sucesss was the intricate staging, which ranged from slick numbers to ultrarealistic but carefully choreographed movements. Without overlooking in the least the contributions of the authors and assistant Bob Avian, here the auteur director-choreographer fully arrived: Michael Bennett. He had (1) admired Jerome Robbins, and (2) spent his choreographic career integrating his dancers into the fabric of the shows he labored on. From the packed bodies of an Upper East Side bar to the secretaries who danced scenic transitions in the business corridors of *Promises, Promises,* from the character- and theme-introducing "Prologue" of *Follies* to the plays he directed (*Twigs* was riotous), Bennett had been honing his style. And when he found the opportunity to work with Broadway dancers—who tend to respond to precise technical demands with ease—as characters, he created one of the American book musical's enduring works of both art and commerce. Bennett strung seventeen separate stories in chronological order for the single book of a dancer's life, and framed it as an audition, to allow the musical to be very presentational as the dancers perform for the director, who conveniently sits behind the audience. Though to the casual viewer *A Chorus Line* has dialogue and monologue, song and dance, in fact every nanosecond of the show was carefully staged and choreographed, right down to at what moment Paul, delivering a long monologue about his life, takes his hands out of his pockets. The cast is required to act, sing, and dance *all at the same time*, and thus we have the perfect integration of musical theatre techniques, made possible by the ascendance of the director-choreographer.

March 1, 1979: *Sweeney Todd.* In a major, masterful, epic score, Stephen Sondheim (again with Hugh Wheeler providing dialogue) pushed beyond musical theatre and comic opera to write what should be described as modern American opera. *Sweeney* had big ideas, big melodies, incalculably incisive lyrics, and a too-big production that crushed the original run, which we shall discuss further on.

And the band played on . . .

By 1980, Broadway had three separate musical genres fighting for attention, almost as if it had returned to the 1920s, when revues, operettas, and giddy musical comedies all drew audiences. The musical comedy was brought back from obsolescence when *42nd*

Street opened on August 25, 1980. Transferring the legendary film to the stage was the modern Busby Berkeley, Gower Champion, who did so with such panache and on such a grand scale. With so many tuneful Harry Warren/Al Dubin songs, with more long-legged beauties than had been seen since the darker *Follies*, and with utter commitment to the melodramatic dialogue by Broadway's last great leading man, Jerry Orbach, modern audiences aplenty didn't just bask in the nostalgia, but thrilled to the glitter and giddiness, the tap dancing and hummability, of the great American musical's oldest format.

Since *Sweeney*, Sondheim has continued to push the boundaries, attempting to define the modern musical as a form in which artistic theories (*Sunday in the Park With George*), irony (*Into the Woods*), sophistication (*Passion*), cynicism (*Assassins*), and a host of other significant ideas and dramatic styles can be incorporated. But increasingly esoteric stories and poor staging has limited his success, along with simple misfires (*Merrily We Roll Along, Bounce*). Still, young, ambitious composers worship Sondheim's seriousness and his sophisticated style, and strive to ape his cleverness.

Others with a more contemporary ear attempt to mimic the success of Andrew Lloyd Webber, whose *Evita* (September 25, 1979) and other poperettas have had enormous commercial, if not critical, success, though the only real American success in the genre to date is *Rent*.

After Michael Bennett died, no director-choreographer rose to take his place, with Tommy Tune, Susan Stroman, and Kathleen Marshall taking Broadway staging back to the clichés from which it came. (Given the paucity of material available, perhaps they cannot be blamed.) Producers, their bravery crippled by rising costs, pandered to tourists and theatre parties seeking brand-name productions. Disney—the elephant in the room, with enough money to bludgeon its shows into shape—sought the widest audience with the lowest common denominator. Rising costs also curtailed the apprentice system, with fewer and fewer stock companies around for young performers and choreographers to cut their teeth on. The success of the English invasion—an entirely different form—pushed the American book musical to the sidelines. The cost of attending live theatre rose so dramatically that the middle class—particularly the artists and writers, students and teachers, and theatre lovers who had attended often—was priced out of regular attendance. Young composers, aware that it takes years to get a single musical on the boards, and a product of their generation, turned away from Broadway to Hollywood, Nashville, and the recording studio. Philanthropic money, which in the 1960s had found art an important part of society, turned to the more immediate response it saw in education and health care, both locally and internationally. And so the story of the American book musical, so long in the writing, while perhaps not moribund entirely, is certainly in transition.

CHAPTER 2

How to Have a Success

"The most important characteristic of a work of art is unity. . . . What we seek are techniques that will increase the harmony among the component parts."
—William Ball, *A Sense of Direction*

Theory: Anything can kill you, but only the score and the staging can put you over the top.

When *Merrily We Roll Along* took to the Alvin Theatre stage for previews, the costumes were a disaster. No sense going into why; few people saw them, because director Hal Prince immediately recostumed the entire cast in tee shirts and sweat shirts that had a description of the character emblazoned on the front, in a (vain) attempt to return the production to the "Hey kids, let's put on a show" concept he began with. That didn't work either, and the show closed after only sixteen now-infamous performances. Since the Stephen Sondheim songs have since become extremely popular, and the show has had greater success in further productions, one could postulate that the costume design killed the musical (and, by extension, the long collaboration of Prince and Sondheim who, after many successful shows, ceased working together again until *Bounce* in 2003).

More than a few musicals have received rave reviews for their sumptuous sets, and pans for everything else (*King of Hearts*). These eye-candy shows closed quickly. "When you leave the theatre humming the scenery," a knowledgeable theatre insider once said, "the show's in trouble." When *Sugar*, the musical version of the film *Some Like It Hot*, opened out of town, the set was considered just too drab for a musical. The musical comedy stumbled through a long pre-Broadway tryout—Washington, Toronto, Boston, Philadelphia—without laughs, but was greeted in New York with a brand new set. It then ran a year and a half, during which audiences were often convulsed.

The wrong set is just as dangerous as the overelaborate or just plain ugly. *Allegro's* set was a substantial, complex series of platforms and turntables that, when the show attempted to come together out of town, lumbered the musical, hampered the staging, and slowed down what should have been a swiftly moving production. (By contrast, *Allegro's* direct descendant, *Stop the World I Want to Get Off*, benefitted enormously from a simple unit set.)

A reunion of performers who have been fired from a musical out of town would be a large gathering of luminaries. Sometimes the role is written out—clearly a sign that the authors didn't have much of a handle on their story in the first place. Sometimes the role changes—same problem—and the performer no longer fits it. Sometimes the promise showed at an audition is never fulfilled. (There is definitely a category of actor whose performance peaks at the audition.) Many times actors who have never sung before are cast in roles requiring singing, among the most famous being Julie Harris in *Skyscraper* and Liv Ullman in Richard Rodgers' *I*

Remember Mama. While the five actors playing the young Marx brothers in the musical *Minnie's Boys* were entrancing—the show was a hit whenever they were onstage—Shelley Winters could not play Minnie (an understatement), a role that had to loom large due not to the story but to her being a star, and the show flopped. What possesses producers to think that a musical muse will suddenly come to these thespians is a mystery. Stars as famous as Ullman can't be replaced or the producer will lose his shirt. Casting can kill you.

Ballroom was Michael Bennett's much-awaited next musical after his mega-success with *A Chorus Line*. Although it featured some of the finest, most entertaining ensemble dance numbers of his career, and a solid, emotional story of a widow climbing back into life, neither of its stars could be considered leading musical comedy performers. Dorothy Loudon was a comedienne extraordinaire, but not a leading lady or polished vocalist. Vincent Gardenia looked like he had neither sung nor danced in his life (and like he didn't want to). Though both were excellent actors who had been outstanding in dramas and comedies, and both brought a wonderful realism to the musical stage, neither could *carry a musical*, and *Ballroom* didn't catch on. (Additionally, its score was by a film and television composer. They tend to write ambient, but not original, theatrical, or melodic melodies.)

Even as *Mata Hari* had only reached the rehearsal stage of a first act run-through, the producer was approached by the writers to fire the director. ("His work was so helpless, so inept, that he had the bulk of the action taking place upstage at a distance far removed from the audience, making the show . . . all but invisible"

(William Goldman, *The Season*). The producer refused, and the show was buried in Washington.

Following their tumultuous experiences of working on Broadway—particularly with David Merrick and Gower Champion—writers Tom Jones and Harvey Schmidt retired to their own small workshop and spent years developing the kind of musical that had established them with the success of *The Fantasticks*. One of those shows—*Celebration*—was moved to Broadway's Ambassador Theatre, where, in spite of a charming score and strong, if dark, allegorical book, it flopped. The writers themselves admitted that the slight, metaphorical, casually costumed and set musical should have been produced Off-Broadway. Even the wrong theatre can kill you. This is also true of *The Grass Harp*, a wonderful small musical lost in the cavernous Martin Beck, often considered by pros as "on the wrong side of 8th Avenue."

Sometimes more than one issue is wrong; a kind of backwards synergy. *Victor, Victoria*, in spite of a luminous and beloved Julie Andrews returning to the stage and a story that had film audiences in stitches, didn't run beyond her personal drawing power. For one thing, the songs simply weren't theatre songs. Film—the derivation of *Victor, Victoria*'s score—can move a song sequence along in many ways, cutting here and there and giving us lots of information beyond the song itself. Onstage, a song has to deliver its impact all alone. *Victor, Victoria* also featured rather cumbersome, old-fashioned staging, sets lumbering in and out. It may even have been in the wrong theatre, the large and cold Minskoff instead of a charming classic Broadway house that might have underscored this charming, old-fashioned show.

In other words, anything can kill you. Costumes, sets, directing. The wrong theatre. Opening numbers (See Chapter Six). Casting.

It would be foolish to claim that everything else about these examples was first-class. On the contrary—*Merrily*'s book is clumsy, snide, and about people we hardly care about. (As opposed to the original Kaufman and Hart play.) *Allegro*'s score did not rise to the romantic passions upon which Rodgers and Hammerstein had become famous. *Sugar* had major structural problems from the get-go. *Ballroom*'s score is a weak pastiche.

But think about it. A musical benefits most of all from synergy, "The action of two or more substances, organs, or organisms to achieve an effect of which each is individually incapable" (*American Heritage Dictionary*). Also: "A chain is only as strong as its weakest link." (A proverb traced back to 1856, just when American musicals were getting under way.) *Merrily* has a wonderful score, one of Sondheim's most accessible. *Allegro* was groundbreaking in its style. *Sugar* boasted a hysterical story (from the film *Some Like It Hot*) and a great comic performance by Robert Morse, and *Ballroom* was helmed by one of the Broadway musical's most astute and creative director-choreographers. In no case was that enough.

Anything can kill you.

Producers are too often seduced by stars who, it inevitably turns out, drag a musical down with their inability to sing, dance, or carry a show: Shelley Winters in *Minnie's Boys*, Mary Tyler Moore and Richard Chamberlain in *Holly Golightly* aka *Breakfast at Tiffany's*, pop concert singer Peter Allen in *Legs Diamond*, magician Doug Henning in *Merlin*, film star Bette Davis in *Miss Moffat*.

Just plain inept writing that couldn't be saved is often the case: *Rachel Lily Rosenbloom and Don't You Ever Forget It, Marilyn, Gantry*, Elizabeth Swados' score for *Doonesbury*, book and lyrics by the otherwise richly comical Gary Trudeau.

Sometimes it's not so inept, it's just that it isn't so good either: *Lovely Ladies, Kind Gentlemen*, and *Sayonara*. A score simply can't be mediocre.

Some adaptations are misguided: a musical version of England's beloved novel *The Wind in the Willows* featured Mole as a woman, and created a love story between Mole and Rat, apparently attempting to avoid the "gay subtext" in the friendship between Mole and Rat (which only gay writers would insist is there). *Dance a Little Closer* attempted to update the time period of the Pulitzer Prize–winning play *Idiot's Delight* from pre–World War II to the future. Lerner, who wrote the book and lyrics, would have been more comfortable in the original time period. (And should have allowed the directors of all his post-Loewe shows to cut, shape, and focus his often long, lugubrious books. Ego can kill you.)

So many musicals utterly lacked directorial creativity: *Look to the Lillies*, *Charlie and Algernon*. Some simply had the wrong director: *Cry for Us All* (Albert Marre), *Home Sweet Homer* (Albert Marre), *Chu Chem* (Albert Marre), *The Conquering Hero* (Albert Marre), *Shangri-La* (Albert Marre), *At the Grand* (Albert Marre) and *La Belle* (Albert Marre). There's also Paul Aaron (*Molly*; *70, Girls, 70*).

While musical theatre director-choreographers tend to make easy and successful transitions to film (Rob Marshall, Bob Fosse, Stanley Donen, Gene Kelly), film directors often find themselves in over their heads directing a stage musical. George Roy Hill tried

Broadway twice: *Henry Sweet Henry* and *Greenwillow*. Vincente Minnelli killed *Mata Hari*.

Some musicals were bad ideas to begin with: *Into the Light* (The Shroud of Turin), *Goodtime Charley* (the relationship between Joan of Arc and the Dauphin of France, while relegating Joan's famous, historic activities to offstage), *A Doll's Life* (sequel to Ibsen's play *A Doll's House*).

Sequels have proved a particularly terrible idea: *Annie 2, Bring Back Birdie*, and *Let 'Em Eat Cake*, a sequel to *Of Thee I Sing*. (Even *The White Fawn* flopped, though it was patterned precisely on the hugely successful *The Black Crook*.)

Producers can panic. (Robert Whitehead fired Bob Fosse.)

Sometimes outsiders make a foolish attempt to conquer Broadway with no previous experience. The notorious mega-disaster *Carrie* was produced by a German businessman, with music by a pop composer, lyrics by a pop lyricist, and book by a Hollywood screenwriter, directed by an English theatre director and choreographed by a television choreographer.

Some musicals suffer expectations they will never fulfill. (*Gone with the Wind*, *Ari* (based on *Exodus*), *James Clavell's Shogun: The Musical* (yes, that's the title).

Librettos are not easy to write. Confusing books sunk *Chaplin* and *70, Girls, 70*, among others. Some productions feature endless, aimless, rewrites (*The Baker's Wife, Dear World*) because no one with a strong vision is in charge. Others grapple unsuccessfully with difficult subject matter, either too dark (*Prettybelle, Lolita, My Love*) or too complex for modest talents (Henry James' *The Ambassadors*).

Period musicals done on the cheap seldom succeed: *Show Me Where the Good Times Are, Onward Victoria*. They deserve luxurious productions. Then there's the operettas whose time had already passed: *Magdalena, Gypsy Lady, Dumas and Son, Zenda* (all produced by the archaic Los Angeles Civic Light Opera).

The really sad cases are the "could have beens." Both *Cry for Us All* and *Goldilocks* deserve resurrection with better direction, and *1600 Pennsylvannia Avenue* featured a great Leonard Bernstein score (when a mediocre one would have still been better than anything else on Broadway) but totally lacked focus, direction, and staging (from four different men).

If you're going to bring a musical film to the stage, you'd better have a stage concept. Lugubrious transfers include *Gigi, Seven Brides for Seven Brothers, Meet Me in St. Louis,* and *Singin' in the Rain.* Turning a great film or play into a musical also requires (1) a good reason, and (2) lyrics as good as the original dialogue. Failures include (but are not limited to) *Sunset Boulevard, Sweet Smell of Success, Georgy,* and *Say Hello to Harvey.* Perhaps unfortunately, the example of *My Fair Lady* will never entirely go away. A great play (*Pygmalion*) *can* be a great musical, but the structure has to be secure, the songs have to rise to the level of brilliance of the play, and the staging has to be breathtaking. Rostand's *Cyrano de Bergerac,* which has had at least three flop incarnations as an English-language musical, will one day be a brilliant musical. As soon, that is, as a great lyricist, composer, and director-choreographer rise to the occasion.

Anything can kill you. Any *one thing* sometimes. After all, if the American book musical has reached the pinnacle of integration— and if it hasn't, there's not much point to this book—then each and every item in it has to do its share.

But there are good shows, and then there are smash hits, the latter a category that popped up often during the golden age. What, then, does it take to make a smash hit?

Music and staging. Each of which deserves a chapter of its own.

CHAPTER 3

The Music That Makes the Show Dance

"True, musical plays need solid scripts. But the first essential nonetheless is a wonderful score. The best parts of a musical occur during the music."
—Ethan Mordden, *Sing for Your Supper: The Broadway Musical in the 1930s*

Here's a list of the composers who wrote a great many songs for Broadway shows, though not operettas, and had at least several hits (one-hit wonders not included; i.e., *Grease*; *Hair*; *Man of La Mancha*; *Promises, Promises*). The dates are not birth-death, but first show-last show on Broadway.

George M. Cohan (1901–1940)
Irving Berlin (1902–1963)
Jerome Kern (1904–1939)
Cole Porter (1916–1956)
George Gershwin (1919–1935)
Richard Rodgers with Lorenz Hart (1919–1943)
Vincent Youmans (1921–1932)
Arthur Schwartz (1926–1963)
Harold Arlen (1930–1959)

Burton Lane (1931–1979)

Kurt Weill (1933–1949)

Frederick Loewe (1936–1960)

Richard Rodgers with Oscar Hammerstein II (1943–1963)

Leonard Bernstein (1946–1976)

Jule Styne (1947–1993)

Frank Loesser (1948–1961)

Cy Coleman (1953–1997)

Jerry Bock (1955–)

Bob Merrill (1957–1972)

Stephen Sondheim (1957–)

Charles Strouse (1960–)

Jerry Herman (1961–)

John Kander (1962–)

The talent to write great original melodies is a strange gift, given to some who are nearly musically illiterate, and often not to those with extraordinary musical skills. Everyone knows by now that Irving Berlin could only play the black keys, and Bob Merrill, who wrote the songs for *Carnival*, *Take Me Along*, and *New Girl in Town* (as well as the smash hit "How Much Is That Doggie in the Window?"), couldn't play an instrument. Yet composers of film scores—long, often classical, background symphonies which they orchestrate themselves—have often failed when called upon to write songs for a musical (*Merlin* and *How Now Dow Jones* by Elmer Bernstein, *Ballroom* by Billy Goldenberg, *Coco* by Andre Previn).

There does seem to have been an outsized group of melodic geniuses among the Tin Pan Alley generation, and well into the golden age. Although not all of them were still writing when the musical reached its fullest integration, all of them contributed to it. Some of them, notably Cole Porter, bridged the styles, writing songs for early musicals and reviews that depended not a whit on the book, and then adapting happily to the book musical. Others grew up in worship of the new musical form. Sadly, with the exceptions of John Kander (b. 1927), Charles Strouse (b. 1928), Jerry Bock (b. 1928), Jerry Herman (b. 1931), and Stephen Sondheim (b. 1930), no one on that list is alive today. Of those five, none are represented on Broadway with an original musical as of this writing.

But it is not my desire to keen over the death of the book musical score. One can hope that more great scores may be written. (Stephen Flaherty and Lynn Ahrens are giving it an honest try: *Lucky Stiff, Once on This Island, My Favorite Year, Seussical, Ragtime.* Stephen Schwartz has had several hits, though all but *The Baker's Wife*, unfortunately sabotaged by the original production, are scores in a pop, rather than theatre, vein.)

The theme of this chapter is the fact that *without* a great score, whatever the style, no musical can succeed to any great extent. Some very weak shows ("book trouble!") have been resurrected due to the attractiveness of their scores. It really doesn't matter to theatre audiences what time period the score represents, so long as it's tuneful, energetic, dramatic, and comedic by turns, and representative of the drama it supports. In 1971 a revival of Vincent Youmans' *No, No, Nanette*, a 1925 musical almost hoary with age, succeeded with modern audiences with an adept combination of tap dancing that hadn't been seen in some time, an "adapted" book, and the star power of a sixty-one-year-old Ruby Keeler giving an invigorating performance. But it was the songs you could hum, going in or going home—"Too Many Rings Around Rosie," "I Want to Be Happy," the excuse-for-a-dance-number songs "You Can Dance With Any Girl" and "Take a Little One-Step," and the timeless "Tea for Two"—that made the show. That same year, the since-then-ubiquitous Andrew Lloyd Webber established his preeminence with *Jesus Christ Superstar*. Though hardly a classic book musical, this rock opera features a very popular score, from the title song to the Dave Brubeck–derived 5/4 song "Everything's Alright" and the melodic ballad "I Don't Know How to Love Him." Webber often proves how far even a few good melodies can take a show.

What makes a great score? Great songs. To be sure, the leit-motifs that integration pulled in from opera helped to sophisticate the musical comedy score. It certainly adds to the drama that, when Paul is carried off with a broken ankle in *A Chorus Line*, not to get the job, "I Really Need This Job" is the underscoring. When Tony's dead body is carried off at the finale of *West Side Story*, our tears are as much triggered by the event as by "There's a Place for Us" in the background. Reprises, underscoring, and musical ideas threaded throughout a score all serve to create so much more than the grab bag of songs that comprised the early musicals. They help create an integrated score. Yet, at the heart of that score is still the songs.

There is no way to define great songs. That's in the "I know it when I hear it" category, an ineffable, unique combination of intervals and rhythm that catches on with the public. Rodgers and Hart's "Blue Moon" didn't, on at least three tries, until Hart rewrote the lyrics as a spoof of moon/June/spoon songs. Go figure. Kern's spectacular "Bill" was cut from at least two musicals before it debuted in *Show Boat*, where it was sung without much context. Although there were underlying themes of unrequited love to support it, many modern directors would not have allowed the insertion of such a blatant stop-the-show-and-sing-a-ballad moment. Their loss.

High marks for music that complements the lyrics, presents the words in such a way that they roll off the tongue in good colloquial style, and enforces the intellect behind them in the expert blending of music and lyrics.

Another strength lies in the cultural nature of the sound; in our case, the very American nature of the songs. As Alec Wilder writes in his seminal book *American Popular Song*:

> Thus, "You've Been A Good Old Wagon, But You've Done Broke Down," composed by the outstanding ragtime pianist Benjamin Robertson Harney in 1895 . . . could not possibly have been mistaken as having come from, say, a London music hall, a *cafe concert* in Paris, a Berlin *musikkafeehaus*, or the *Theatre an der Wien* in Vienna.

By the same token, if in reverse, American composers have written enchanting songs with foreign influence. *Cabaret* is rich with Weill's Weimer period, *Man of La Mancha* with Spain.

One thing certain is the talent of those golden age composers to write not just a few good tunes, but a full score. So many recent scores feature only one or two good songs—generally in the "power ballad" genre—and the rest is filler. Here is the song list for Frank Loesser's *Guys and Dolls*:

> "Fugue for Tinhorns" ("I got the horse right here . . . ")
> "Follow the Fold" (the Salvation Army appears)
> "The Oldest Established" ("crap game in New York")

"I'll Know" ("when my love comes along")

"A Bushel and a Peck" (Hot Box Girls onstage, Act One)

"Adelaide's Lament" ("A person could develop a cold")

"Guys and Dolls" (one of the all-time great theme songs)

"If I Were a Bell" (the heroine falls in love)

"My Time of Day" (the hero's theme)

"I've Never Been in Love Before" (the hero admits)

"Take Back Your Mink" (Hot Box Girls onstage, Act Two)

"More I Cannot Wish You" (advice to the lovelorn)

"Luck Be a Lady" (gambler's lament)

"Sue Me" (comic classic for a classic comic)

"Sit Down, You're Rockin' the Boat" (gospel scene)

"Marry the Man Today" (Finale, message)

Any fan of musical theatre, or popular songs, can surely hum more than half of those without prompting. So many hits. So many different songs. And all within the context of the book.

And that, of course, is the key, for surely music gains from having a dramatic skein behind it, as much as drama gains from having the right music supporting it.

Too many of today's composers write one or two great melodies, and the rest is padding. Too many scores are primarily pastiche. Added to the ability to write an authentic, original score is the ability to write with some variety within an overall style. *West Side Story* features bebop, Latin, vaudeville, songs with syncopated rhythms, soaring ballads, and complex contrapuntal scenes. The last two were based on the same song, "Tonight," first done as a yearning love ballad, and then as the tense, driving "Tonight Quintet." Yet no one would accuse the score of being a hodgepodge.

My definition of "score," however, is a collection of interconnected songs. Nothing wrong with reprises, leitmotifs, contrapuntal singing, underscoring et al. But it's the *songs* that carry the musical. Today, the preponderance of a terrible need for sophistication, (which is itself a misreading of the scores of Kurt Weill, Leonard Bernstein, and Stephen Sondheim) combined with a dearth of melody, has led us to the "sung-through" score, an excuse for lazy writing. Here is the master of the modern musical, Stephen Sondheim, on the subject:

> To write a thirty-two bar song that has freshness and style to it and tells the story is really hard. And nobody does it anymore. Everybody writes so-called "sung-through" pieces, and it's because anybody can write sung-through pieces. It's all recitative, and they don't develop anything, and it just repeats and repeats and repeats. And that's what most shows are. I don't even go see the shows; it's so boring to me.

Randall A. Byrn, writing on blogcritics.org on July 22, 2006 about *Spring Awakening*, a new musical based on the 1891 play by Frank Wedekind, loves the dichotomy of nineteenth-century school boys rockin' and rollin' . . .

> The young actors are dressed as teenage German schoolboys in the 1890s, sitting rigidly in Latin class. Their frustration with the demands and insults from their strict schoolmaster is evident. Then one of the boys reaches into his jacket pocket, pulls out a wireless mike, and begins to belt out a vivid and very twenty–first century pop-rock song. The other boys pull out their own mikes and join him. It's a startling moment, exhilarating, thrilling. And many of the musical numbers that follow are also brilliantly staged and pulsing with energy. They provide some of the most exciting performances I've seen onstage in some time.

Yet clearly the same critic didn't become emotionally engaged enough to give the show a positive review . . .

> The idea of juxtaposing Frank Wedekind's famous play about adolescent repression and rebellion from more than a century ago with a contemporary, rather *Rent*-like rock score is aesthetically bold. I wish I could say it was more than that. But once the plot and characters begin to become clear, the production becomes progressively less interesting. The dialogue (excerpted from the original) and the songs, for the most part, don't add to each other or comment on each other—they seem to exist on different planes, and *the whole is much less than the sum of the parts.* [my italics]

Thus the production's failure to capture the very essence of the great American book musical: synergy. Nevertheless, *Spring Awakening* has been a success, will undoubtedly be performed by teens through the world for years to come, and represents the new Broadway. No art form remains static.

This sentence was in the opening paragraph of the June 16, 2006 *New York Times* review by Charles Isherwood of the same musical.

> . . . it is disorienting to find the nineteenth-century German school-boys in the new musical *Spring Awakening* yanking microphones from inside their little woolen jackets, fixing us with baleful gazes and screaming amplified angst into our ears.

Only disorienting? *Jesus Christ Superstar*, in which microphones and amplified angst burst out of biblical times, had opened on Broadway in 1971. There isn't anything new about the rockeretta, though some are better (*Rent*) and some are worse (*Rockabye Hamlet*), and entertainment hasn't any boundaries. But Wagner wouldn't approve. He wouldn't like the fact that, after a century of development to reach the peak of integration, of his *gesamt-kunstwerk*, we had abandoned it in the blink of a rock chord.

Still, lamentations that rock music has pushed theatre music out of the limelight have been going on for twenty-five years now, ever since, well, ever since it did. But not having songs that U2 wants to cover should not be a handicap to a musical. Yes, it was a great help to the economics of the theatre when Broadway scores sold well, and cover recordings by popular singers helped publicize the show. Probably the last time a single recording helped a show so much was Streisand's "People" from *Funny Girl* in 1964, the same year that Dean Martin and The Beatles jockeyed for the number one spot on Billboard's Top 100. But plays have survived centuries without the help of "auxiliary rights," or a recording by Frank Sinatra, and the golden age musicals, and the form itself, should also. The right music for the drama is every bit as important as the pure quality of the songs.

Sometimes the right singer can put a song over. Often people who cast musicals are forced to make a last-minute choice for a leading role between a good actor who sings only fairly well, and a good singer who acts only okay. An outstanding example of a very quixotic choice is the original casting of Tony and Maria for *West Side Story*. Two very operatic voices were in the final running: Frank Porretta and Anna Maria Alberghetti. As were two dancers with little experience: Larry Kert and Carol Lawrence. The latter were cast. The production gained immeasurably from the *authenticity* of the two good but not operatic singers, who were the right age for the roles, and had the raw voices of youth. A 1990 recording of *West Side* featuring opera singers utterly demolishes the drama behind the musical, in favor of big, operatic voices that would be entirely out of place in Hell's Kitchen.

A good hook, of course, can help. Interesting harmonics. Unique intervals.

Perhaps not the latter. Herewith, a Jule Styne story that may very well be apocryphal, yet given Jule's personality and the fact that he told it to me personally, has the ring of authenticity. He and his collaborators were agonizing over the casting of Sydney Chaplin in their musical *Bells Are Ringing*, when Jule complained, vociferously—a normal speech pattern for the dynamic personality— that Chaplin had only three notes to his range, and would be hard to write for. As evidence, Jule pounded those three notes on the piano repeatedly, shouting, "that's all he has, these three notes, just these three notes, that's all he can sing . . . " then, looked down at his fingers, he created the melody to "Just in time, I found you just in time, before you came my time, was running low . . . "

A good song may be hard to spot when you first hear it. Theatre legend Irving Berlin played and sang a freshly written song for a famous theatre director. The director couldn't imagine that it was any good. Then he got an idea. "Irving," he said, "sing 'Always.'" One of Berlin's greatest hits. Berlin did, and when it sounded equally as awful in Berlin's reedy monotone, the director understood, and the new song was in.

A great score may be hard to define, but you've got to have one if you want to mount a good musical. A variety of songs (please, not two hours of power ballads), including comedy (even in *West Side Story* we get "Gee, Officer Krupke"). A smooth blending of music and lyrics. All arising strictly out of the high emotional points in the story. Melody, syncopation, and harmony rooted in the time and place of the drama. Character-driven.

And that undefinable, ineffable something that makes the songs original, unique . . . great. You'll know it when you hear it.

Before we go on to the second element—staging—that is crucial to the success of a book musical, let's examine where these songs come from. This is the heart of the composer.

CHAPTER 4

The Lyricist: Sung Hero of the Broadway Musical

"Nobody listens in the theatre anymore, and it's because everybody is so used to miked sound that they don't have to concentrate."

—Stephen Sondheim

Reacting to Beethoven, Wagner felt that music alone could never become expressive enough. He needed a libretto. He remarked that even Beethoven used language in his *Ninth Symphony*.

A legendary theatre story goes like this: Mrs. Oscar Hammerstein was at a party, and overheard someone say, "I just love Jerome Kern's 'Old Man River.'" Mrs. Hammerstein replied, "Jerome Kern didn't write 'Old Man River.' My husband wrote 'Old Man River.' Jerome Kern wrote, dum, dum, dum-dum, dum-dum, dum, dum-dum."

So to give them their due, here's a list of lyricists who created the golden age. While composers Cohan, Berlin, Porter, Herman, and Sondheim supplied their own lyrics, these men and women supplied lyrics for hundreds of shows and thousands of songs. Again, dates are first Broadway show to last Broadway show.

P. G. Wodehouse (1905–1935)

Ira Gershwin (1918–1946)

Lorenz Hart (1919–1943)

Oscar Hammerstein II (1920–1959)

Howard Dietz (1924–1963)

Dorothy Fields (1928–1973)

Yip Harburg (1929–1968)

Alan J. Lerner (1943–1983)

Betty Comden and Adolph Green (1944–1991)

Sheldon Harnick (1958–)

Lee Adams (1960–)

Fred Ebb (1965–1997)

When Rodgers wrote with Hart, he generally wrote the music first. When he wrote with Hammerstein, the lyrics generally came first. Although no sane adviser would ever argue for one way over the other, the fact is that the difference between Rodgers and Hart's method and Rodgers and Hammerstein's marks the transition from songs tossed willy-nilly into a musical comedy, and a theatrical score. For the book musical, lyrics began to need more than the cleverness of Gilbert, Wodehouse, and Hart. They needed broader ideas, drama and comedy, pithiness, and character. It became so much easier to write the lyrics first than to try to force them to fit an existing melody.

One day at an audition for a female singer, a particularly good one interrupted the usual lethargy of those listening, and Jule Styne, arguably Broadway's greatest living composer at the time, jumped up and shouted, "You know why she's so good! Because she sings the lyrics, not the melody!"

Now remember, Styne was a composer, not a lyricist. Yet he was always ready to expound upon the idea that a great singer was great because he or she got behind *the idea of the song.* Sang *the words* with passion and authenticity. It was, he claimed (during the same tirade), just what made Ethel Merman and Barbra Streisand great, both great singers for whom he had written their greatest scores. Listen to their recordings. Two more divergent deliveries you couldn't imagine. But with this one thing in common: a passion for the words or, more precisely, the ideas behind the words.

Here it is put another way by the actress Dame May Whitty to her daughter Margaret Webster (from Webster's memoir, *The Same Only Different*):

> "You will be told," she would say, "that you have a beautiful voice. So you have; the credit is God's, not yours. But whenever you hear your beautiful voice making a beautiful noise . . . change it." She meant, of course, to guard me against the danger of falling in love with a mellifluous flow of sound at the expense of inner truth.

Perhaps opera buffs are listening for the tone of that high C, the trills and vibratos of the well-trained voice. Not the rest of us. Popular music and theatre songs are alike in this. We want to be touched with the emotion of the song. Can anyone doubt that Roy Orbison is yearning for that pretty woman walkin' down the street, when they hear his perennial hit for the umpteenth time? It wasn't just Sinatra's mellow tone that made him the most popular vocalist for those private romantic moments. He made us believe in what he sang about. When Merman planted her feet center stage and sang, "For me! For me! For me!" it wasn't the note that caught the audience in the gut. It was the passion with which she proclaimed it.

No one can deny that a great song requires a great voice. If the singer is off pitch, or the tone dull or thin, all but the most tone-deaf members of an audience will wince. That, however, is simply because flat notes are *distracting*. They take us out of the moment, away from the idea. If a character is supposed to have a great passion—and most leading characters should, or where's your plot strength?—he or she needs a voice to match. If you don't have a great sound on the high note that tops Billy Bigelow's "Soliloquy," you're going to let us down. But the note, so big and rich and round, can't, on its own, thrill audiences. It needs passion behind it. We might look back on those days and see John Raitt and Alfred Drake as rather stiff compared to the subsequent descendants of the Actors Studio, but let us allow for the culture and style of the time. If an actor playing Billy Bigelow today has to be far more realistic—and he does, or the production will be seen as old-fashioned at best and boring at worst—that only goes to say that the actor, no matter the vocal difficulty, must be utterly believable delivering the strongest of emotions.

And those emotions are supplied by the lyricist.

Best definition of a song: "Words deliver an idea to the head. Music delivers an emotion to the heart. A song delivers an idea to the heart" (Ira Gershwin). Also phrased as, "Words make you think thoughts, music makes you feel a feeling. A song makes you feel a thought" (Yip Harburg). Who said it first is lost to history.

While librettists might plan a spot for a song, it is ultimately the lyricist who has to sketch the words. And where those words come in the story, and what they're about, is just about the *single most crucial thing there is in the writing of a book musical.*

Let's get the very obvious out of the way first: in a musical, the audience is expecting music. You can't go too long without song or dance. I don't know what the longest spate of dialogue is in a musical, but I would bet that more than ten minutes without music, and the audience is going to get pretty fidgety.

Pearl Bailey thought so. There's a substantial dialogue scene in *Hello, Dolly!* when Cornelius and Barnaby meet Irene and Minnie in the hat shop. It's a costume change for Dolly. When Bailey played her, she often came sailing back into the shop as soon as she was changed, seldom waiting for her cue. She would ad-lib to the audience the plot points she had skipped over, and launch into the "Motherhood" number. The authors hated it. The audience loved it.

Yet it's not enough to say, "We've got too many pages of dialogue here; let's throw in a song." Neither is it enough to structure the rhythm of the show carefully, though that is certainly important, and more than one show has been improved enormously with the addition of a song during tryouts. The first key to the success of a musical is this: *what are the songs about?*

From *1776*, here is one of the most unique, original sets of theatre lyrics ever written.

Songs 1, 2, and 3: Three tunes in a row form the opening—"Sit Down, John," in which John Adams demands a yes vote on independence, the Congress clearly refuses, and the long, hot summer is invoked ("Someone ought to open up a window— no, too many flies"); "Piddle, Twiddle, and Resolve," in which Adams complains of Congress's recalcitrance; and "Till Then," in which John and Abigail Adams—singing their letters, for she is at home—claim their separate needs (John: "Saltpeter!" Abigail: "Pins!") and establish their longing for each other. Before a word of dialogue is uttered, much is established: time and place, character, conflict.

Song 4: Next, Benjamin Franklin inveigles Richard Henry Lee from Virginia to go home and get a resolution from his state calling for independence, to introduce to Congress, so it won't come from the "obnoxious and disliked" Adams. Lee, in a showstopping number vaguely in the "want song" category (though it's what Adams wants), explains that of course he will get it, as "The Lees of Old Virginia," "the oldest family in the oldest colony," are reliable. Before leaving, he does enough encores to drive the impatient Adams crazy.

Song 5: Now the new declaration must be written. "But Mr. Adams," say Benjamin Franklin, Thomas Jefferson, Roger Sherman, and Robert Livingston, his colleagues in favor, "you are obnoxious and disliked." For it to get a fair hearing in Congress, surely someone else must write it.

Song 6: "Yours, Yours, Yours"—wherein John and Abigail Adams tell each other what's happening—creates a romantic moment, briefly releasing tension from the debate.

Song 7: Jefferson is convinced to write it, but is getting nowhere. Adams sends for Jefferson's wife, with the hope it will cure his writer's block. She arrives, spends the night, and the next morning—as they wait impatiently to see if it worked—Martha Jefferson tells Benjamin Franklin and John Adams that Thomas

Jefferson, well, "He Plays the Violin." Really well. (Innuendo. One of the great love songs in musical theatre.)

Song 8: The biggest obstacle to declaring independence comes from the "Cool, Cool, Considerate Men," of Congress, led by John Dickinson, who expound a philosophy key to conservatism: that "most men with nothing would rather protect the possibility of becoming rich than face the reality of being poor." Their stately gavotte ("to the right, ever to the right") underscores their intransigence in the face of progress, their fear of change, their loyalty to England's King.

Song 9: In one of the most moving anti-war songs ever written for the theatre, a courier from the front, singing about a mother looking for her dead son on the ghostly battlefield, sings "Momma Look Sharp."

Song 10: Upon arguing over whether the symbol of the new United Colonies should be a turkey or an eagle, Benjamin Franklin, John Adams, and Thomas Jefferson are waiting for "The Egg" to hatch.

Song 11: Representative Edward Rutledge, arguing for the excision of a proposed anti-slavery clause in the Declaration, explains the hypocrisy of the colonies as they benefit economically from the "Molasses to Rum to Slaves" trade.

Song 12: Finally, in one of the most stirring of soliloquies, John Adams—desperate to gain the votes necessary and utterly convinced of the rightness of the cause—demands, "Is Anybody There?" Whereupon he turns and goes inside for the final vote, by which time—amazingly, since we know the outcome—we are nevertheless on the edge of our theatre seat.

You won't hear those songs on the radio, but each one is so rich in the play's textural ideas, so well blended in, many think of *1776* as a play with music.

Where do such great ideas for songs come from? The book. But who finds them? The obvious answer is the lyricist. (Though he may, of course, be open to suggestions from his composer, the librettist, or anyone else at a production meeting courageous enough to throw in an idea.)

Here is an extraordinary solution to the problem of finding a song for a pivotal scene in *Pygmalion*, to be turned into *My Fair Lady*: Professor Higgins is trying to teach Eliza how to speak proper English. She tries. And tries and tries. They seem to be getting nowhere. They are about to give up. And then she gets it. Celebration. The celebration becomes a song, an exuberant tango. The lyrics are simple and repetitive. "I think she's got it!" They repeat her success on the phrase "The rain in Spain," and throw in a few "Hartfords" and "Hampshires" for the bridge. You probably think, simple. But like all great ideas, it wasn't so simple before someone else thought of it. In fact, it's brilliant, because it is the *highest emotional moment of the sequence* for the characters. Their enthusiasm for their own success makes them ebullient, a natural mood from which to launch into song and dance. As our sympathy is with Eliza, we celebrate with her, and the song is just what we need at the moment to satisfy our emotions. The emotions are derived directly from the story, and the song has taken the characters to an emotional level they *could not attain with dialogue alone.*

Because Lerner was one of the preeminent lyricists of the American theatre, because it was thought by so many that *Pygmalion* could not be musicalized, and because *My Fair Lady* is one of the best-written musicals in theatre history, let's look at the structure of the musical, compare it to the source, and see where Lerner found inspiration for musical numbers. With this comparison, we can also see just how adaptation is accomplished, for no matter how great the original source, a dozen or more moments worth musicalizing might not all be found in the original text.

Pygmalion	*My Fair Lady*
Act I: Covent Garden; 11:15 p.m. "Torrents of rain. Pedestrians running to take cover."	Act I, Scene 1: "Outside the Royal Opera House, Covent Garden; a cold March night. Richly gowned, beautifully tailored Londoners exit the opera as costermongers warm themselves around a smudge-pot fire. Three buskers (English street entertainers) perform, then pass the hat."

Lerner and Loewe here follow Rodgers and Hammerstein's *Oklahoma!* breakthrough, dispensing with a full company opening number in lieu of introducing the main characters and getting the plot under way at once. They use *Pygmalion's* crowd scene—operagoers milling about—to create a colorful stage picture, and then proceed to the story. Although most director/choreographers cannot resist a rousing opener (see Chapter Six), *Fair Lady* was directed by Moss Hart. ("Torrents of rain" probably proved impractical.)

Pygmalion	My Fair Lady
In the pouring rain, Freddy Eynsford Hill fails to get a cab for his mother and sister, but manages to bump into Eliza Doolittle, spilling her flowers.	Freddy runs into flower-selling Eliza, but ignores her to search for a taxi.
Eliza approaches Colonel Pickering to buy flowers.	Eliza approaches Colonel Pickering to buy flowers.
Professor Henry Higgins is seen writing in his notebook, and is mistaken for a policeman. He amazes the crowd by identifying their various ancestral neighborhoods. The rain stops, and all exit except Pickering, Higgins, and Eliza.	Professor Henry Higgins is seen writing in his notebook, and is mistaken for a policeman. He amazes the crowd by identifying various ancestral neighborhoods.
Pickering and Higgins meet, recognize each other as linguists. Higgins explains his profession. ("You see this creature with her kerbstone English: the English will keep her in the gutter to the end of her days.") He explains that, by teaching her how to speak properly, he could "pass her off as a Duchess at an Ambassador's garden party." They go off to have supper. As they leave, Higgins leaves money for Eliza's flowers.	Pickering and Higgins meet. Higgins describes his talent, and complains how the English mangle their language. At last the first song: "Why Can't the English?" (With its comical list of how well other nationalities behave in this regard, one could imagine its prototype was Noel Coward's lyric: "Only mad dogs and Englishmen go out in the noonday sun.")
Freddy returns with a cab at last, only to find Eliza taking it with the coins Higgins left her for flowers.	

Having stuck pretty close to the content of Shaw's opening sequence, with the insertion of the busker's entertainment at curtain rise and one song based solidly on Shaw's idea, Lerner and Loewe now begin to move further from Shaw, without ever leaving him completely.

Pygmalion	My Fair Lady
	Alone, Eliza and the costermongers dream of a better life. Lerner and

Pygmalion	My Fair Lady
	Loewe here provide Eliza's "want song": "Wouldn't It Be Loverly?"
	On Tottenham Court Road, Eliza's father gets ejected from a pub, but Eliza comes by and he cadges half a crown from her. This leads him to expound upon his philosophy of life. Song: "With a Little Bit of Luck."

Lerner and Loewe have greatly increased the role of Eliza's father, Alfred P. Doolittle, with two rousing music hall songs, one in each act.

Pygmalion	My Fair Lady
Eliza comes to Higgins, offering to pay for speech lessons. Higgins takes up a bet with Pickering. In six months he can pass her off as a lady. Mrs. Pearce takes Eliza off to get her cleaned up.	Eliza arrives, offering to pay for speech lessons. Higgins makes a recording of her accent. The bet is on. Mrs. Pearce takes Eliza off to get cleaned up.
Higgins explains to Pickering: "I find that the moment I let a woman make friends with me, she becomes jealous, exacting, suspicious, and a damned nuisance. I find that the moment I let myself make friends with a woman, I become selfish and tyrannical. Women upset everything. When you let them into your life, you find that the woman is driving at one thing and you're driving at another . . ."	Higgins explains to Pickering his bachelor's philosophy. Song for Higgins: "I'm an Ordinary Man" ("But let a woman in your life. . ."), obviously inspired by Shaw's wonderful paragraph. (The song ends with brilliant staging: Higgins turns on all his recording equipment, and the room is filled with piercing female babble.)
Mrs. Pearce returns, and asks Higgins to watch his language and manners as long as the girl is with them. (This particular theme—that Higgins often uses profanity, which annoys his mother—is eliminated from the	Tottenham Court Road. Doolittle, once again ejected from a pub, hears the news: Eliza has moved in with a swell. This bodes well for the old man, so he reprises his philosophy. ("With a little bit of luck, someone else will do the bloomin' work. . .")

Pygmalion	My Fair Lady
musical, though his abrasiveness and lack of manners are very much kept alive.)	
Doolitle goes to Higgins, intending to extort money from Higgins. Higgins calls his bluff, threatens him. Doolittle retreats, but suggests five pounds, and rationalizes his difficult position. ("I'm the undeserving poor.") Higgins, delighted with the man's eloquent philosophy, gives him the five pounds. (He turns down ten, it would make him feel too prudent, and he couldn't spend it on a spree.) As he leaves, he barely recognizes Eliza coming in.	The mail includes an invitation from an American millionaire philanthropist for Higgins to lecture to a Moral Reform League.
	Doolittle appears, thinking to extract the five pounds, etc. Upon leaving, he almost doesn't recognize Eliza, who comes in, frustrated from having to say her vowels all day. Finding Doolittle to be eloquent on the subject of morals (he can't afford them), Higgins tells Mrs. Pierce to urge the American to book Doolittle for the lecture.
	As for Eliza's exhaustion, Higgins has no sympathy, and leaves her to practice her vowels.
	Alone, she imagines what she'll do to her tormentor. Song: "Just you wait, 'enry 'iggins." If a picture is worth a thousand words, in a musical, a song is worth a thousand lines of dialogue when it digs deep into the character. Lerner and Loewe here expand on Eliza's difficult journey from cockney to lady by allowing her to vent her frustration.

And now Lerner and Loewe insert a remarkable sequence. While in Shaw's version the next scene jumps to Eliza's first test with the public, for the musical we see the journey: Eliza's lessons, her frustration at endless practice, and, ultimately, her triumph.

Pygmalion	*My Fair Lady*
	Blackout. Lights up. Eliza still practicing, now with Higgins and Pickering trying to help.
	The servants appear, feeling sorry for Higgins. Song: "Poor Professor Higgins!" A good time-passing conceit.
	Back to practicing. Higgins and Pickering share pastries, Eliza looks on longingly.
	Servants again, singing.
	Back to Eliza, Higgins, Pickering. Higgins pops marbles into Eliza's mouth, referring to Demosthenes.
	Servants again, singing. ("Quit, Professor Higgins!")
	Back to Eliza, Higgins, Pickering. All are exhausted. Light indicates it's morning. But suddenly she's got it! Song: "The Rain in Spain."

As already remarked, here we have a textbook example of finding the right idea for a song: atypical, unique, not hit-parade stuff, but perfect for the drama of the scene. And who would have thought there was a popular song in the emotion of this scene? Not Rodgers and Hammerstein, not Dietz and Schwartz. Not Yip Harburg nor Fred Saidy, not Cole Porter nor Frank Loesser, all of whom turned down *Pygmalion* as impossible to *musicalize*. Lerner saw one.

Pygmalion	*My Fair Lady*
	With success, Higgins suggests they take Eliza to his mother's box at the Ascot races. Then Higgins and Pickering go to bed, leaving

Pygmalion	*My Fair Lady*
	Eliza to practice. The sensible Mrs. Pearce suggests she go to bed as well. But Eliza is far too excited at her own success. Song: "I Could Have Danced All Night." There is here something developing in Eliza's relationship to Higgins, quite subtle, but heard far louder than in the play. ("I only know when he/Began to dance with me. . . .")
	(Upon examination, it does seem a bit odd that Eliza sings "I Could Have Danced All Night," in celebration of her success with her language lessons, as opposed to later in the story, upon returning from the Embassy Ball, where she succeeded with her entire impersonation, and where she danced.)
Mrs. Higgins drawing room. Henry arrives, to his mother's consternation, as it is her day to receive visitors, and she knows they "stop coming whenever they meet you." (In the preliminaries we have a neat Shavian line to his mother, and one simply ringing of Freud: "My idea of a lovable women is something as like you as possible.")	
Freddy's mother and sister arrive, the sister flirting with Higgins, despite his abominable manners.	
Pickering arrives. Freddy arrives. And finally Eliza arrives. She has transformed into a lady, and in fact is ravishing to Freddy. She speaks well, though with a bit of the old slang. ("My aunt died of influenza . . . But it's my belief they done the old lady in.")	

Pygmalion	My Fair Lady
Eliza leaves. Mrs. Eynsford Hill, her daughter, and her son Freddy leave. Mrs. Higgins warns her son Henry and Pickering that they have created a problem: what to do with Eliza when they've created a lady. They hardly worry, believing they can find her a position in a flower shop.	

Note that Lerner and Loewe have cut Freddy's mother and sister from the musical altogether.

Pygmalion	My Fair Lady
	Outside Ascot. Pickering warns Higgins' mother that Higgins will be bringing a flower girl to the races.

Here Lerner and Loewe "open up" the musical, opting to go to Ascot itself, rather than the home of Mrs. Higgins, for Eliza's first test.

Pygmalion	My Fair Lady
	Inside a club tent, Ascot. The stage is filled with ladies and gentlemen, whose excitement over the thundering horses is highly tempered. Song: "The Ascot Gavotte" ("Ev'ry duke and earl and peer is here. . .").

Now Lerner and Loewe really strike out on their own, as there is nothing like this scene or its ideas in the play. The stately, stuffy upper class move so slowly and precisely in the musical sequence that Eliza's coming enthusiasm will be a stirring contradiction.

Pygmalion	*My Fair Lady*
	Henry arrives, meets his mother. Eliza and Pickering arrive. Eliza "produces an impression of remarkable distinction and beauty." Eliza meets Mrs. Higgins' friends, including Freddy, who is instantly smitten. Mrs. Higgins, warned by her son that Eliza's two topics are the weather and "how do you do," is helpful, steering the conversation toward the weather.
	The race gets underway. The crowd is stately, but Eliza can't help cheering for her horse, and brings down the curtain (and the house) with "Move your bloomin' arse!!"

Some productions of the musical end the first act on that famous line, though originally Act I went all the way to the Embassy ball.

Lerner and Loewe not only place Eliza's entry into the upper classes onstage—in the play it takes place offstage—but they do it three times: first when she visits Mrs. Higgins, here at Ascot, and finally at the coming Embassy ball. In the play it happens only once.

Pygmalion	*My Fair Lady*
	Outside Higgins' house, Wimpole Street. Freddy, besotted with Eliza, knocks on Higgins' door and delivers flowers. Though Eliza won't see him, he's deeply in love, and thus perfectly happy to wait "On the Street Where You Live."

Here Lerner finds an original approach to an age-old musical theatre moment: "I'm in love." The character of Freddy, like Doolittle, has gained a great deal in the musical translation. They have also written one of the all-time "in one" numbers; its purpose, to change the scenery.

Pygmalion	*My Fair Lady*
	Higgins' study; six weeks later. They're all going to the Embassy ball. Pickering urges Higgins to call it off, worried Eliza will be discovered and embarrassed. Higgins refuses. She appears in her new gown, and is ravishing. A wonderful moment for the audience, as we've been rooting for her from the start. Even Higgins manages to reverse character and offer his arm to her as they exit. The bet between Higgins and Pickering depends upon this evening.

The promenade of the Embassy, "in one," so we can change the scenery again. Guests arrive. Ominously, Zoltan Karpathy, Higgins' former phonetics student, who uses his talent to blackmail people trying to hide their origins and who will be Eliza's true test, arrives. Pickering arrives and informs Higgins' mother that things are going well. We discover that Mrs. Higgins has grown "terribly fond of that girl," indicating that she and Eliza have developed, if offstage, a nice relationship.

The full stage set having been changed, we go inside the ballroom of the Embassy, where we begin with the show's only real dance number, an energetic waltz known to the cast as "Hanya Holm's |

Pygmalion	*My Fair Lady*
	Hernia Hop." As with all well-written musicals, the dance has a plot: Higgins dances with Eliza, but Karpathy makes his way closer and closer to them until, when everyone is supposed to change partners, he captures her. They dance, they talk. They talk so animatedly they stop dancing. Higgins decides to do nothing, but watch and see what will happen. And all continue dancing as the curtain (in the original) descends in suspense: will she or won't she be discovered?
Higgins' study. Midnight. Higgins, Pickering, and Eliza come home. Pickering to bed. Higgins can't find his slippers. Eliza throws them at him. She is terribly angry they have taken all the credit for her successful transformation. She's also worried about what she can do now, since she is hardly fit to go back to selling flowers on the street. When Higgins finally understands, he tells her she does have options. She could get married. We get a dash of the class system: Eliza: "I sold flowers. I didn't sell myself. Now you've made a lady of me, I'm not fit to sell anything else."	They arrive home in great triumph. Pickering explains that they succeeded. Song: "You Did It." The servants chime in with congratulations. Higgins is looking for his slippers. Eliza throws them at him. We notice, if no one onstage does, that Eliza doesn't say a word. In fact, she is furious. When the servants and Pickering have gone off to bed, Eliza turns on Higgins. She is angry they have taken the credit, and worried over what will become of her now. She can't go back to her former life.
Eliza demands to know whether the clothes and jewels are hers; she doesn't want to be accused of stealing when she leaves. She gives back a ring he bought her. Losing his temper over her ungratefulness, he angrily throws it across the room and retires.	When Higgins finally understands, he tells her she does have options. The scene then develops as in the original, until Higgins throws the ring and leaves. Alone, Eliza vents her anger. Song: "Just you wait, Henry Higgins . . ."—this time singing her Hs properly!
She imitates his angry exit, and then returns to look for the ring.	On the street. (In one.) Eliza, suitcase in hand, exits the house, only to find Freddy still waiting for her. He professes his love, but she's had

Pygmalion	*My Fair Lady*
	enough of words; she wants action. Song: "Show Me" ("Don't talk of love. . .Show me!"). But of course, as he tries, she just gets angrier, tossing him about until finally she bops him with her suitcase and marches off alone. Clearly, it isn't Freddy that she hopes will show her his love. Thus have Lerner and Loewe greatly intensified, primarily with songs, the relationship between Eliza and Higgins.
	Eliza returns to the costermongers at the flower market, but they don't recognize her.
	Her father comes out of the pub, dressed for a wedding. It seems that when Higgins recommended Doolittle to the American philanthropist as an original moralist, the man left him thousands of pounds in his will, making Doolittle "respectable," which has caused his live-in to insist on marriage. Doolittle is appalled—though not so much that he would give the money back.
	Freddy appears, having been waiting in a taxi. Eliza realizes this life is no longer hers, and goes off with him, leaving Doolittle to his last few hours of bachelorhood. Song: "Get Me to the Church on Time."
Mrs. Higgins, drawing room. Higgins and Pickering come in, complaining to Higgins' mother that Eliza has bolted. They tried the police, but the police made insinuations about the propriety of the relationship. Mrs. Higgins reminds them that Eliza has every right to leave.	Still home, Higgins' is upset that Eliza has bolted. ("The girl belongs to me! I paid five pounds for her!") He wonders why women can't be more like men. Song: "A Hymn to Him." ("Why can't a woman. . .Be like me!") Pickering exits to the Home Office to elicit some help. Higgins leaves to visit his mother.

Pygmalion	My Fair Lady
	But Eliza, already there, explains to Mrs. Higgins that after her success at the ball, Higgins and Pickering took all the credit, and no notice of her. Mrs. Higgins is quite sympathetic.
Doolittle arrives, well-dressed, and complains that he's been left a substantial annual bequest by an American philanthropist, with the only request that he lecture at the Moral Reform League. Turns out that Higgins mentioned him to the millionaire. Now Doolittle is expected to be respectable, and support his relatives.	

So Lerner and Loewe have simply moved this idea forward a bit, and managed out of it to glean their second, showstopping music hall number for Doolittle.

Pygmalion	My Fair Lady
Eliza comes downstairs, carefully elegant. She thanks Pickering for his treatment of her, and explains that without the example of his manners, she would not have known how to behave. She explains that Higgins' manners and language were terrible. She can't go back now. "I have forgotten my own language, and can speak nothing but yours. That's the real break-off with the corner of Tottenham Court Road."	Henry arrives, startled to find Eliza, who treats him with exaggerated civility. He paces back and forth in the rear, "gnashing his teeth," while Eliza explains to Mrs. Higgins about her son's awful treatment of her.
Mr. Doolittle explains that he's marrying his live-in and invites Mrs. Higgins, Pickering, and Eliza to the wedding. All exit except Eliza and Higgins.	

Pygmalion	*My Fair Lady*
Alone, Higgins and Eliza argue over his treatment of her, and he confesses that he "has grown accustomed to her face." Shaw's scene—one of the best in dramatic literature—has her arguing for some kindness, and him explaining that he treats everyone the same way. She finds him cold. ("I'll marry Freddy, I will, as soon as he's able to support me." "I'm not going to have my masterpiece thrown away on Freddy.") With Eliza's future up in the air, all but Higgins go off to Doolittle's wedding. The curtain comes down with Higgins expecting her to return to him. (In a written note to the script, Shaw says she marries Freddy.)	Mrs. Higgins exits to see the vicar, unwilling to let him into the same room as her son. This leaves Higgins and Eliza to one of the best written "love" scenes in theatre. ("The question is not whether I treat you rudely, but whether you ever heard me treat anyone else better," and "I'll marry Freddy, I will, as soon as I'm able to support him.") Exasperated, she finally lets him know that she can do very well without him. Song: "Without You." ("There'll be spring ev'ry year without you.") Then she walks out, to Mrs. Higgins, applause.
	Higgins, alone, and in another unique approach to a standard moment, admits that he's in love with her. Song: "I've Grown Accustomed to Her Face."
	(This song is also done "in one," in order to change the set back to . . .)
	Higgins' study. Higgins turns on the gramophone and sadly listens to the early recordings of Eliza's voice. She returns. He fails to rush to her; it isn't in his character. Nevertheless, he accepts her in his own way. He says quietly: "Eliza, where the devil are my slippers?"

Let's catalogue what Lerner and Loewe have done:

1. Although they have trimmed Shaw's dialogue significantly, they have not eliminated a single plot point or idea!

2. Some ideas they clearly found in Shaw have been turned into songs: "Why Can't the English?," "I'm an Ordinary Man," and "You Did It."

3. They have staged Eliza's transformation and her success, where Shaw left both offstage. We see her practicing, at first futilely, and then with some improvement, until she gets it: "The Rain in Spain." Then we see her at a small social gathering, and then a large social gathering—good for the chorus number "Ascot Gavotte"—and finally at the ball, good for a dance number, "The Embassy Waltz."

4. They have expanded the roles of both Freddy and Doolittle. They allow Freddy to moon over Eliza, a natural for a love song, "On the Street Where You Live." And they give Doolittle two rousing music hall ditties, his philosophy ("With a Little Bit of Luck"), and, where Shaw has him getting married, the entertaining, "Get Me to the Church on Time." Both songs allow Doolittle to lead his cronies in rousing staging.

5. In fact, with those two songs and "The Embassy Waltz," "Ascot Gavotte," and the costermongers helping Eliza with "Wouldn't It Be Loverly?" Lerner and Loewe have made room in the story for the ensemble, while keeping them integrated into the fabric of the show.

6. Most useful of all, they have given both leads songs that enrich their characters. Eliza, when she sings "Wouldn't It Be Loverly?" (her "want song"), is clearly setting out a desire we will soon see she has the gumption to achieve. Her anger at Higgins' treatment is clear in "Just You Wait," which, in the hands of a

skilled actress, also lets us know that the relationship is not so simple as it seems. Higgins, in "A Hymn to Him," lays down his English bachelor's philosophy.

7. And finally, Higgins capitulates—if not directly to her, to us, in the show's second love song, "I've Grown Accustomed to Her Face." Not again until Sondheim ("You're always sorry, you're always grateful . . .") will love be stated in so truthful, eloquent, and sly a way.

8. And of course, unlike the play, Eliza returns to Higgins. Although in his written epilogue to the published play Shaw claims that Eliza marries Freddy, Lerner's own remarks in the published musical are equally famous (and far more satisfying): "Shaw and heaven forgive me, I don't think he's right." In fact, Mrs. Patrick Campbell, the first to play Eliza, didn't agree with Shaw either. On opening night, when, upon leaving Higgins for the last time, she was asked by Higgins to buy him a pair of gloves, she turned in the doorway and ad-libbed, "What size?" At that point, according to Lerner's memoir, "the curtain fell, and so did Shaw's jaw."

All in all, it's a textbook example of turning a play into a musical, and one that might well have fallen short, given the density and brilliance of the original. Each song takes an emotion within the character to higher dramatic levels than it could achieve without music. Every significant scene *includes* a song. The songs are well-balanced, varying genres, with only one ballad.

And each song is quite specific to the character who sings it.

Let's take a quick look at just how much more specific songs have become. Here's a list of songs from *Very Good, Eddie*, an early Princess Musical (1915):

"We're on Our Way"
"The Same Old Game"
"Some Sort of Somebody"
"Isn't It Great to Be Married"
"Wedding Bells Are Calling Me"
"On the Shore"
"If I Find the Girl"
"Thirteen Collar"
"Old Boy Neutral"
"Babes in the Wood"
"The Fashion Show"
"I Wish I Had a Million"
"Nodding Roses"

And here are the song titles from Frank Loesser's 1961 *How to Succeed in Business Without Really Trying*:

"How to Succeed"
"Happy to Keep His Dinner Warm"
"Coffee Break"
"The Company Way"
"A Secretary Is Not a Toy"
"Been a Long Day"
"Grand Old Ivy"
"Rosemary"
"Cinderella Darling"

"Love from a Heart of Gold"

"I Believe in You"

"Brotherhood of Man"

Even though the Princess Theatre trio was working hard to integrate their songs, unlike the early Kern/Wodehouse songs, most of Loesser's songs for *How to Succeed* are so show-specific as to be nearly useless in any other setting.

In fact, one difficulty in keeping the American songbook alive is that, while the early Tin Pan Alley songs by Cole Porter, the Gershwins, and others can be sung in many contexts (ASCAP lists over eighty different recordings of "I Got Rhythm"), the modern musical contains many songs that make no sense out of context. Good for the show. Bad for the composer's royalties.

On the other hand, too much writing—too many songs—can hurt the book musical.

I have written elsewhere that the decline of the American musical began with the success of *Annie*, because that musical, however wonderful the idea, lacked craft to an extraordinary degree. Despite Strouse's tuneful songs, the lyrics are mundane, the book dull—though not the story for tots—the staging flat. Even the original performances, each great in their own way, ranged over a variety of incompatible styles—the antithesis of the cohesiveness the American musical had arrived at by the golden age.

Now I believe that the downfall might have begun even earlier, with *A Little Night Music*. Not due to a splendid production of an incandescent score, but due to the fact that ever since then, young composers have attempted to ape Stephen Sondheim but succeeded only in copying the complexity of his work and not the inspiration. Subsequent scores have been filled with leitmotifs, arch cleverness, trios and quartets, and contrapuntal writing, but none have the originality or flat-out tunefulness of "Send in the Clowns," "A Weekend in the Country," or "The Miller's Son." A score has to be tuneful. Tune full. A score has to include *songs*.

Singing every plot point in a story reduces the effectiveness music can have on the stronger emotional moments in favor of a singular pattern without high points. If Billy Bigelow were singing his heart out all through *Carousel*, where would he go with "Soliloquy?" If John Adams had been singing his praises (literally) of the Declaration of Independence for days already, how could his penultimate frustration be such a great moment ("Is Anybody There?")? Even today, these book musicals offer much greater emotional catharsis than *The Light in the Piazza, Rent, Les Miserables*, and others of their ilk.

Which is not to say that these poperettas and rockerettas are not entertaining. On the contrary, audiences seem very impressed with all three examples of the sung-through musical. But entertainment is not drama. The theatre that touches our hearts is more than entertainment. It is, dare I say it, uplifting, and thus a vital contribution to a civilization's culture.

One of the most powerful moments in any musical is the "Quintet" from *West Side Story*. Five characters or sets of characters (the Jets, the Sharks, Tony, Maria, Anita) each sing their own lyrics to a tune we've already heard ("Tonight"), each with their own hopes for the coming evening. Only the audience, knowing them all, sees a train wreck coming. Certainly the soaring Bernstein melody carries *an idea to the heart.*

If the music alone must touch us for your show to be a success, it's the lyrics that inspire the music. And it's the ideas behind the lyrics that cause the moment to work within the musical. Which brings us to . . .

CHAPTER 5

At the Heart of It All: The Libretto

"The success or failure of a show is settled when somebody says, 'Wouldn't it be a great idea . . .'"
—Howard Lindsay

When Bock and Harnick were asked of their songwriting which came first, the music or the lyrics, Bock replied at once: "The book." (This anecdote is also attributed to Sondheim.)

While film is best as a story told through actions, theatre profits more from ideas defined by language. Wagner felt that it should be the emotions, not the events, that precipitate the climax.

Thus the great strength of the modern American book musical is the drama behind it, because that's what all the separate pieces are built upon.

And the key to the book is this idea:

Characters become too charged for speech, and in the songs the emotional action moves forward. (Richard Eyre and Nicholas Wright, *Changing Stages: A View of British and American Theatre in the Twentieth Century*)

Nobody could say it better.

Pity the poor book writer, though. You never read about "Arthur Laurents' *West Side Story*," or "Sam and Bella Spewack's *Kiss Me Kate*," or "Richard Stilgoe's *Phantom of the Opera*." Yet when a show goes awry, it's nearly always book trouble.

Book problems have been blamed for a number of failures in the modern era. This, however, has been nearly simultaneous with the rise of the song as mini-drama; the Sondheim-esque song so rich in character and drama that it brings more to the table than the dialogue, and eventually *overshadows* the book. This conundrum arrived with *Follies*, in which Sondheim's songs brought so much to the characters that the James Goldman libretto was barely a framework. It continued with Sondheim's *A Little Night Music* and *Sweeney Todd*, in which dialogue is little more than connective tissue. Aficionados of *Follies* think the book is weak, and wrong-headed attempts have twice been made to solve this with rewrites. There are only twelve songs in *Oklahoma!* There are twenty-two musical sequences in *Follies*. What little time was left for Goldman was simply not enough for him to develop ideas. Thus it is probably no coincidence that the modern musical often has more "book problems" than the classic musical. The increasing use of song and dance in modern musicals has created difficulties for the librettist. A good structure isn't enough. The scenes need to be as concise as the lyrics, as emotional as the melodies, and as well-staged as the choreography. It's a tall order for playwrights who, dazzled by the idea of writing a musical, find themselves out of their element.

What is the libretto for a musical? Two things: story structure and dialogue.

Story structure includes the ideas for the songs, and whether these ideas are contributed by the bookwriter, songwriters, director, choreographer, producer, or even the lighting designer; doesn't matter, as long as the story includes enough emotional moments of enough significance to the characters to require singing or dancing. That is the essence of the book musical, that *the story provides characters whose psychological journey regularly reaches the point where words are simply not enough*. When we set about looking for a story—original or existing—to musicalize, that is what we should be looking for: moments in the plot line that cry out to be raised to the level of emotion only music can provide.

Alan Jay Lerner explains that in writing *My Fair Lady*, he and Loewe continued to come up with ideas "until we arrived at those moments where music and lyrics could reveal what was implied and not repeat what was already in the text, and could catch the drama at the hilltops where it could ascend no further without the wings of music and lyrics. . . ." There is no better description of where to place songs within a libretto. (It was their general method to come up with a title and idea for a song; Loewe would then write the melody, and then Lerner would finish the lyric.)

To return to "The Rain in Spain" from *My Fair Lady*, the scene begins with dialogue. Eliza, Higgins, and Pickering are exhausted and frustrated, for Eliza, after hours of practice, is still saying, "The rine in Spine is minely in the pline." Then, just when you think she isn't going to get it, she does. "The rain in Spain is mainly in the plain!" This breakthrough calls for a celebration. The exuberance of the characters fairly cries out for music and dance.

If, however, you were to set the entire sequence to music, as in the "sung-through" musical entertainments so popular in the last few decades, you have no arc of emotion. If you sing, "The rhine in Spine," you have nowhere to go for "The rain in Spain." This, then, is the principal difference between the book musical and the poperetta: the former provides an arc of emotion with which to arrive at the song. We ride that arc with the character and exult as he/she does. We have the character's emotional catharsis along with them. In the latter, we simply applaud all that singing. Poperetta is the refuge of the composer who cannot write a dozen great songs for a show (as in Irving Berlin's *Annie Get Your Gun*, Jule Styne's *Gypsy*, or Frank Loesser's *Guys and Dolls*), but only a few melodies and lots of padding.

While standing ovations were originally spontaneous outbursts of emotion that translated into bravos as the bows took place, it seems to me lately that we are applauding the technique alone. We bravo the fact that the cast got through three hours of singing with lots of high notes. We are impressed, but we seldom have the emotional experience that great musical theatre once offered. Even in as simple and entertaining a book musical as *Hello, Dolly!*, when, in the end, Dolly looks up to heaven and speaks to her first husband about her newfound happiness, we feel happy too. It's been a long (and extremely entertaining) journey, but it's been an emotional one as well.

With most of the significant moments in the story given over to song and dance, dialogue (the other half of the librettist's job and the half that he labors over alone) then becomes significant in a number of other ways. It has to set up a sequence that leads to the music. It has to be entertaining on its own (or we're just waiting for the next number). It has to signal traits, so we know something about the characters. Most of all, it has to give us a subtle sense of anticipation, of suspense. Something has to be building to the (musical) payoff.

Librettists have to go into the enterprise knowing that their best, strongest writing will be subsumed by the lyricist and turned into a song. Sometimes the very lyrics will have been theirs in prose form. They have to face the fact that their scenes will not be whole without the songs. If they were, we wouldn't need the songs at all. They have to be willing to write a great story, and then give up all the great parts to their collaborators. There are very few writers with the awkward combination of creative urge and self-effacing personality required to be the book writer of a musical.

It was Arthur Laurents' willingness to give over large sections of his libretto to the songwriters and the choreographer that ultimately allowed *West Side Story* to become such a fully integrated, fluid musical. In fact, it was Laurents who suggested that the opening could better be done in dance than in a dialogue scene among the Jets, which he had written. It was another page of prose Laurents had written about Tony that became the lyric "Something's Coming." These are the sacrifices of the librettist.

The librettist's greatest responsibility is the invisible thread that holds it all together. Call it . . .

Structure

"The best musicals have a thrilling seamlessness and a cumulative emotional charge; the worst are lumps of dialogue interleaved with musical interludes." (Eyre and Wright, *ibidem*)

Before musical comedy had evolved to musical theatre, songwriters could insert their melodies nearly anywhere. "Structure" was as simple as not having too many ballads in a row, not going too long without a song (or without the girls in the chorus), and the ordinary requirements of the well-made play, such as a good act climax. Credit Guy Bolton, as far back as the Princess Theatre musicals, with trying to make the songs flow out of his scenes. By the modern age, however, when songs had to grow organically out of the dramatic text and had to grow from the emotions of the characters (who should have reached the point in their scenes where only singing or dancing could adequately express the way they felt), a songwriter depended heavily on the story. (Thus the increased value in adapting a musical from a proven play, or other source.)

Though good scenes are important, the real talent a book writer needs is in structuring a musical.

Peter Stone, ace librettist and notorious book doctor on many shows, said to Marty Bell (for *Broadway Stories*, Limelight, 1993): "A musical is all structure. When the structure works, the show works; when the structure doesn't work, the show doesn't work." And: "Without structure nothing will work—not the songs, not the dialogue, not the characters. You can fix all those in rehearsal in no time at all. But if you don't have the structure right, whatever fixing you do on the other things, the musical simply is not going to work." Or, as William Goldman recorded in *The Season*, when Sheldon Harnick listened to the umpteenth version of a scene that wasn't working, he shook his head sadly and said, "The trouble with washing garbage is that when you're done, it's still garbage."

More than two-thirds of the musicals produced on Broadway throughout the twentieth century were adaptations, with an increasing number from the golden age when, presumably because of the new form, songwriters were increasingly relying on tried and true material. Plays are by far the most popular, but novels, short stories, and biographies have all been successfully (and just as often unsuccessfully) adapted. Possibly the most unusual is *A Chorus Line*, adapted from the true life stories of a number of Broadway dancers, as told in a series of recorded interviews. Here are the sources for most of the musicals that are on our "landmark" list in Chapter One, between 1943 and 1975.

Oklahoma!: Adapted from the play *Green Grow the Lilacs*.

On the Town: Adapted from the one-act ballet *Fancy Free*, but primarily an original.

Carousel: Adapted from the play *Liliom*.

Kiss Me, Kate: Adapted from Shakespeare's *The Taming of the Shrew*.

South Pacific: Adapted from James Michener's interconnected short stories, *Tales of the South Pacific*, particularly "Fo' Dolla" and "Our Heroine."

Guys and Dolls: Adapted from Damon Runyon's Broadway stories particularly "The Idyll of Sarah Brown."

The King and I: Adapted from the novel *Anna and the King of Siam*.

Threepenny Opera: Adapted from *The Beggar's Opera*.

The Golden Apple: Roughly adapted from the *Iliad* and *Odyssey*.

Peter Pan: Adapted from the play by James M. Barrie.

My Fair Lady: Adapted from George Bernard Shaw's play *Pygmalion*.

The Most Happy Fella: Adapted from Sidney Howard's play *They Knew What They Wanted*.

West Side Story: Adapted from Shakespeare's *The Tragedy of Romeo and Juliet*.

Gypsy: Adapted from the memoirs of Gypsy Rose Lee.

The Fantasticks: Adapted from the play *Les Romanesques* by Edmond Rostand.

How to Succeed in Business Without Really Trying: Adapted from the book of the same name.

A Funny Thing Happened on the Way to the Forum: Based loosely upon the Roman comedies of Plautus.

Hello, Dolly!: Adapted from Thornton Wilder's play *The Matchmaker*.

Fiddler on the Roof: Adapted from the stories of Sholom Aleichem, particularly "Tevye and His Daughters."

Man of La Mancha: Adapted from Cervantes' classic Spanish novel *Don Quixote*, which Dale Wasserman, the librettist, had already adapted into a successful television play.

Sweet Charity: Adapted from the Fellini film *Nights of Cabiria*.

Cabaret: Adapted from the play *I Am a Camera*, by John van Druten, and the Berlin stories upon which it was based, by Christopher Isherwood.

Promises, Promises: Adapted from the film *The Apartment*.

Jesus Christ Superstar: Loosely adapted from the Bible.

A Little Night Music: Adapted from the Bergman film *Smiles of a Summer Night*.

Raisin: Adapted from the play *Raisin in the Sun*.

Chicago: Adapted from the 1926 play of the same name.

Original librettos, though fewer, are the foundation of more great musicals.

Allegro: Original, unsuccessful.

The Music Man: Original.

Bye Bye Birdie: Original.

Funny Girl: Original, though based on the life of Fanny Brice.

Hair: Original.

Company: Original, though based on a dozen unproduced playlets.

Follies: Original.

Pippin: Original.

A Chorus Line: Original, developed from interviews with dancers.

Whether adaptation or original, story structure is crucial. Let's examine two extremely strong structures. First . . .

West Side Story

It was Montgomery Clift who brought *Romeo and Juliet* to the attention of Jerome Robbins. Robbins introduced the idea to Bernstein and Laurents, and the two settled on *East Side Story*, setting the love story between a Jewish boy and a Catholic girl. Other projects kept this one from moving forward until Arthur Laurents, noticing a newspaper headline about the ethnic enmity between West Side gangs in Manhattan, suggested refashioning the idea and the geography. Career timing aside, I believe it was this idea that ignited the imagination of the authors and propelled them forward.

Laurents then made a very straightforward translation of the classic Shakespeare play *Romeo and Juliet*. He renamed but kept almost every major character, eliminating only the parents (Maria's father has a line or two from offstage).

The Capulets	become	Puerto Ricans/Sharks
The Montagues	become	Whites/Jets
Romeo	becomes	Tony

Juliet	becomes	Maria
Mercutio	becomes	Riff
Prince	becomes	Lt. Shrank
Friar Lawrence	becomes	Doc
Nurse	becomes	Anita
Tybalt	becomes	Bernardo
Paris	becomes	Chino

Here is a comparison between the source and the musical of one of the best "books" of an extremely well-integrated book musical:

Romeo and Juliet	West Side Story
The houses of Capulet and Montague fight. The Prince stops them, and warns that he will no longer put up with these brawls that disturb the peace ("If ever you disturb our streets again. . .").	The two gangs fight. "Prologue." Lt. Shrank arrives to stop them. ("You're gonna make nice with them PRs from now on. Because otherwise I'm gonna beat the crap outta every one of ya and then run ya in.")
	Riff, a Jet, proposes a war council with the Sharks to agree on a fight that will settle once and for all who controls the territory. "Jet Song."
Romeo is in love with Rosaline, but it is unrequited. Benvolio advises him to look for another girlfriend.	Riff convinces Tony to come to the dance. Tony has a premonition: "Something's Coming."
Paris is a suitor for Juliet. Capulet, her father, agrees, and offers to give a feast where they might meet. Lady Capulet urges Juliet to look on Paris "with admiration."	Anita is preparing Maria's dress for the dance. Bernardo and Chino come in. Chino is to take Maria to the dance.
Romeo, Mercutio, and Benvolio go to Capulet's feast wearing masks.	

Romeo and Juliet	West Side Story
Romeo sees Juliet and falls in love. Tybalt recognizes the voice behind the mask. It's a Montague! But Capulet says they're acting like gentlemen, let them stay. Tybalt exits angrily. Romeo and Juliet realize they are from feuding families.	"The Dance at the Gym." Tony meets Maria. Bernardo comes between them. A war council is set for later. Tony sings "Maria."
Romeo avoids Mercutio and Benvolio. They exit.	
The famous balcony scene. Romeo and Juliet profess their love, agree to marry and to meet tomorrow. Romeo goes to Friar Lawrence for help.	Tony comes to Maria, who appears on the fire escape. They profess their love ("Tonight").
	Puerto Rican boys and girls argue about America versus Puerto Rico. The boys leave. The girls sing "America."
Friar Lawrence collects herbs and weeds for medicine. Romeo asks for help.	
Mercutio and Benvolio are looking for Romeo because Tybalt has sent a challenge.	While the Jets wait for the Sharks for the war council, Riff urges them to play it "Cool."
Juliet's Nurse arrives. Romeo sends a message through Nurse for Juliet to meet him at Friar Lawrence's cell.	The Sharks arrive. Tony arrives, reduces the proposed fight to one on one with fists only. Shrank arrives and wants to know where it's going to be, but nobody says.
Nurse tells Juliet to go to Friar Lawrence.	
Romeo is impatient, Juliet arrives. Friar Lawrence marries them.	Tony comes to the dress shop to meet Maria. Anita realizes why he is there. Maria and Tony sing "One Hand, One Heart." Tony agrees to try to stop the fight.
	The "Tonight" quintet. All sing of their excitement about the coming

Romeo and Juliet	West Side Story
	evening: Jets and Sharks about the rumble, Tony and Maria about meeting each other, Anita about seeing Bernardo.
Mercutio, Benvolio, and the Montagues meet Tybalt, Petruchio, and the Capulets. Tybalt wants a confrontation. Romeo arrives, Tybalt insults him. Romeo walks away. Mercutio draws on Tybalt. Tybalt draws. They fight. Romeo holds Mercutio back, but Tybalt stabs him under Romeo's arms. Romeo challenges Tybalt. They fight. Tybalt is killed. Benvolio urges Romeo to flee.	The "Rumble" begins, Bernardo versus Diesel. Tony tries to stop it. Bernardo hits Tony. Riff fights Bernardo with knives. Tony tries to stop them, but in doing so, blocks Riff from seeing Bernardo, who kills Riff. Tony kills Bernardo. Anybodys urges Tony to flee. Maria and her girlfriends prepare for a night with the boys after the rumble. Maria says, "I Feel Pretty."
Juliet, waiting impatiently, is told by Nurse that her cousin Tybalt has been killed by Romeo. Juliet is torn, but worried more about Romeo than sorrowed by Tybalt's death. Nurse agrees to take a message, and her ring, to Friar Lawrence for Juliet. Nurse enters, gives Romeo Juliet's ring, and promises to tell Juliet that Romeo will come to her. Capulet promises Paris he can marry Juliet in three days.	Chino arrives. He tells Maria that Tony has killed her brother, gets a gun, and leaves. Tony arrives. He and Maria sing "Somewhere." A "dream ballet," denoting such a place for all, takes place.
Romeo and Juliet meet. She urges him to go to Mantua, as he has been banished. He does. Lady Capulet and Capulet tell Juliet she is to be married soon to Paris. She refuses. Friar Lawrence gives Juliet a potion that will make her appear to be dead. The family will place her body in their mausoleum. Then he	The Jets gather, make fun of Officer Krupke ("Gee, Officer Krupke"). Jets go to look for Tony before Chino finds him.

Romeo and Juliet	*West Side Story*
and Romeo will come to her as she awakens, and Romeo and Juliet can run away together to Mantua.	
Capulet arranges the wedding. Juliet agrees to marry Paris.	
Juliet drinks the potion.	
Capulet, preparing for the wedding, tells Nurse to go wake Juliet.	
Nurse, Lady Capulet discover Juliet "dead." Friar Lawrence consoles the family.	
There is a comic scene between musicians preparing for the wedding.	
Romeo waits for news. Balthazar enters, tells him that Juliet is dead. Romeo buys poison from a local apothecary.	Tony and Maria have slept together. Tony leaves through the window as Anita arrives. Anita tries to tell Maria about "A Boy Like That," but she says "I Have a Love."
Friar Lawrence finds that his letter to Romeo warning him of the plot did not reach him. Lawrence hurries to the tomb.	Anita warns Maria that the Sharks are looking for Tony, and Chino has a gun.
	Shrank arrives at Maria's apartment, looking for Tony. Maria sends Anita to the drugstore to warn Tony.
	Anita, nearly raped by the Jets, lies and tells them that Maria was killed by Chino.
	Doc tells Tony that Maria is dead.
Paris hides. Romeo arrives. They fight, Paris is killed. Romeo drinks the poison, dies. Juliet awakes, sees Romeo dead, stabs herself. Everyone arrives to survey the tragedy.	Tony runs into the playground and shouts for Chino to come and kill him. Chino finds him, and does. Everyone appears. Maria blames everyone for her brother and Tony's deaths. The Jets and the Sharks carry Tony's body off together.

While the musical's ending is no less of a tearjerker, it isn't a true tragedy. Maria lives. Nevertheless, very few fundamental changes were made to the story. The genius is in the transliteration and the musicalization.:

1. In the play, we first meet Romeo as he moons over Rosaline, an unrequited lover. He drops her the moment he sees Juliet. (And is criticized as fickle by Friar Lawrence.) In the musical when we meet Tony, he is not yet in love at all, simply anxious for something to happen in his life ("Something's coming, I don't know what . . . ").

2. In the play, Friar Lawrence is part of the problem, secretly marrying the young lovers, and then helping them to a solution that, in fact, is the cause of their death. Although Doc does take the erroneous message to Tony, he does so innocently, thinking that Anita has told the truth.

Although the film version of *West Side Story* is probably the single most faithful film ever made of a Broadway musical, three changes were made for the screen:

1. In the musical, following the scene in which the Puerto Rican boys and girls argue about the value of coming to America, the boys leave, and the girls sing "America" themselves, primarily Anita versus Rosalie. In the film, the boys stay, and the number is done boys versus girls, a major change for Robbins, who extended the choreography into a wonderful dance sequence on the roof.

2. The positions of the songs "Gee, Officer Krupke" and "Cool" are reversed. In the stage version, the tense "Cool" comes in Act One, in the drugstore as they wait for the Sharks to hold a war council, while the comical "Krupke" comes in Act Two, following the rumble. The filmmakers use "Krupke" up front, and then "Cool" in the rumble's aftermath. In fact, Sondheim originally wanted it that way in the stage version, but Laurents argued against it. The film proved Sondheim correct.

3. The dream ballet "Somewhere," defining the world as it should be, is not used in the film version, though the song is.

1776

It was Sherman Edwards who first wrote the book of *1776*, along with the music and lyrics. Much dialogue and ideas came from authentic writing from the period, Edwards having been a history teacher. When Stuart Ostrow optioned it for production, he convinced Edwards to relinquish the libretto to Peter Stone (whose two previous musical books were *Kean* and *Skyscraper*). Stone did some significant editing and structuring—he was probably the best at that since Hammerstein—but his two greatest contributions, according to his own recounting, are the calendar on the wall and the scoreboard. The latter allowed the audience to keep track of how far from "unanimous" (required) the Continental Congress was from signing the Declaration of Independence, and the former created a "ticking clock." They worked in tandem. *Will they make it?* Surely everyone in the audience knew that the Declaration of Independence was signed on July 4. Yet *1776* manages to create *suspense.* How in the world will this recalcitrant, obnoxious, disparate group of Representatives ever agree on anything, much less the most important document ever created in American history?

And that tidbit only partially accounts for the success of *1776*: an original musical, based on nothing but history, of transcendent artistic success (and commercial success, as it happens).

The authenticity of the dialogue and the plot points is another reason. No musical presents real, historical events more accurately, more specifically than does *1776*. In an afterward to the published libretto, the authors go to great lengths to define where they altered, merged, or overlooked various events. In brief: the weather *was* unusually hot and humid, with a bumper crop of horseflies due to the stable next door ("Someone ought to open up a window! No, no, too many flies"); John Adams described himself as "obnoxious and disliked"; Jefferson did indeed play the violin; the Declaration was debated for three full days—eighty-six separate changes were made, and over 400 words deleted, including those that called for the abolition of slavery; and Caesar Rodney of Delaware did have skin cancer, appearing in public with a green scarf wrapped around his face, and did indeed ride the 80 miles all night in great pain in order to break the deadlock in the Delaware delegation. These and many other character issues and events (Washington's dispatches were constant and extremely gloomy) have been incorporated into the drama to great success.

Changes that were made (none of which "have done anything to alter the historical truth of the characters, the times, or the events of American independence."—*the authors*) include the following: Independence was declared to the citizenry on July 4. The congressional vote, however, had come on July 2, *after which* the document itself was debated and amended. The document was actually signed over a period of several months thereafter. The authors built the debate to the signing for a brilliant dramatic climax, which led to the brilliant staging of the finale: an imitation of the Pine-Savage painting, in which the actors approached the document and froze, and the scrim in front of them lit up with the document itself. And Jefferson, who was indeed pining for his wife, probably visited her in Virginia. There is no record that she came to Philadelphia. The authors invented this to maintain the unity of place.

Two scenes were eliminated out of town, both illustrating the trip that Adams, Franklin, and Chase made to New Jersey to inspect the military—a trip that in actual fact Adams and Franklin took after, not before, the vote on independence. One scene was at an inn, in which Franklin and Adams had to share a bed; the other on the military training grounds. In the interests of both length and symmetry of setting, both were cut. Clearly, the drama of the debate in Congress had gained a great grip on the audience, and to veer too far from it was unnecessary. Additionally, the unit set, so much of the musical taking place within the Congressional Hall (along with the weather), added a claustrophobia that created dramatic tension.

One additional interesting factor: "The action is continuous. There is no intermission." Well, maybe on Broadway. Unfortunately, those shows that have been successful without an intermission— *Follies*, *A Chorus Line*, *Man of La Mancha*, and *1776*—are generally required to suggest a possible halftime for subsequent productions, as local producers tend to hate the intermissionless entertainment.

If you know that movie theatres make most of their profits on concessions, you know why. There's also the iron butt factor. Too many people heading out for a restroom break. Selling those souvenir programs and merchandise.

The most experienced writers and directors in the business are often confronted with weaknesses in the structure of a musical almost as soon as the show previews. The out-of-town tryout in a chaotic atmosphere, traditional for a century of Broadway musicals, was essential in order to cope with often extensive changes. The financial and logistical difficulties of pre-Broadway bookings have led to readings, workshops, regional and stock productions, and other substitutions for Washington, Boston, Philadelphia, Detroit, and New Haven. But one way or another, the director-choreographer is more than ever responsible for seeing that the authors have their ducks in a row. Otherwise, no amount of great staging will carry the day.

A unique way to analyze a dramatic structure is to compare it to "The Hero's Journey," which was synthesized by Chris Vogler from the work of famed mythologist Joseph Campbell (*The Hero with a Thousand Faces*). According to this approach, the hero's journey has twelve stages:

1. Ordinary World: The hero's normal world before the story begins.

2. Call to Adventure: The hero is presented with a problem, challenge, or adventure.

3. Refusal of the Call: The hero refuses the challenge or journey, usually because he's scared.

4. Meeting with the Mentor: The hero meets a mentor to gain advice or training for the adventure.

5. Crossing the First Threshold: The hero leaves the ordinary world and goes into the special world.

6. Tests, Allies, Enemies: The hero faces tests, meets allies, confronts enemies, and learns the rules of the Special World.

7. Approach: The hero hits setbacks during tests and may need to try a new idea.

8. Ordeal: The biggest life-or-death crisis.

9. Reward: The hero has survived death, overcomes his fear, and now earns the reward.

10. The Road Back: The hero must return to the Ordinary World.

11. Resurrection Hero: Another test where the hero faces death—he has to use everything he's learned.

12. Return with Elixir: The hero returns from the journey with the "elixir," and uses it to help everyone in the Ordinary World.

Let's look at the structure of *Funny Girl*, a musical that, ironically, had enormous book problems and went through dozens of drafts, several directors and choreographers, and two famous feuds. One was between producers David Merrick and Ray Stark; the other between Stark and composer Jule Styne, before resulting in a smash hit and launching the career of twenty-one-year-old Barbra Streisand. (In this case, our hero is a woman.)

In *Funny Girl*, Fanny Brice, just a girl from Brooklyn (Ordinary World), wants to go on the stage (Call to Adventure), but isn't your ordinary beauty (Refusal of the Call). Nevertheless, with a little help from the choreographer (Meeting with the Mentor), she gets into vaudeville (Crossing the First Threshold). In spite of numerous difficulties (Tests, Allies, Enemies) she becomes a star (Approach), attracting the attention of a handsome man (Ordeal) who ultimately marries her (Reward). Unfortunately, he turns out to be a gambler and, ultimately, a thief (The Road Back), but she manages to say goodbye with dignity (Resurrection), and go on with her life (Return with the Elixir).

Pretty darn good for a musical with book trouble!

Moreover, each of these important touchstones has a song that exploits it: proof that the authors eventually found the strongest emotional moments in the story to musicalize.

1. Ordinary World: "Henry Street"

2. Call to Adventure: "If a Girl Isn't Pretty"

3. Refusal of the Call : "I'm the Greatest Star" ("but no one knows it")

4. Meeting with the Mentor: "Who Taught Her Everything She Knows"

5. Crossing the First Threshold: "Cornet Man"

6. Tests, Allies, Enemies: "I Want to Be Seen With You Tonight." Also, Ziegfeld doesn't want her to be funny.

7. Approach: "His Love Makes Me Beautiful" (She's funny anyway) and "Don't Rain on My Parade"

8. Ordeal: "You Are Woman" ("I Am Man")

9. Reward: "Sadie, Sadie" and stardom: "Rat-Tat-Tat-Tat"

10. The Road Back: "Who Are You Now?"

11. Resurrection: "The Music That Makes Me Dance"

12. Return with Elixir: "Don't Rain on My Parade" reprise

Although not all the songs here are in the same order as the journey, almost every stage has its equivalent song.

Let's do it again with *Pippin*, another musical for which the writers got less credit than they deserved, due to the slick staging of Bob Fosse.

1. Ordinary World: "Welcome Home"

2. Call to Adventure: "Corner of the Sky"

3. Refusal of the Call: "War Is a Science"

4. Meeting with the Mentor: "Magic to Do"

5. Crossing the First Threshold: "On the Right Track"

6. Tests, Allies, Enemies: "Glory"

7. Approach: "Simple Joys" and "No Time at All"

8. Ordeal: "With You"

9. Reward: "Morning Glow"

10. The Road Back: "Extraordinary"

11. Resurrection: "Love Song"

12. Return with Elixir: Finale

There's another structural requirement in good musicals, and that's the type of musical number presented. There should, in the American book musical, be a variety. Too many of today's musical entertainments (*Rent, Wicked*) feature a score that consists almost entirely of power ballads. Too many ballads in a row will bore an audience. Too many dance numbers will be repetitive. Again, Alan Lerner: "There are also conventions in the musical theatre: conventions involving the balance of the score, the proper distribution of solos, ensemble singing, and choreography. What is exciting is to be aware of these conventions and use them for fresh expression. It is not enough that there be a fast song after a slow song. Legitimate, dramatic ways must be found so that the character or characters arrive at the emotional moment that demands the right kind of music to balance the score."

Let's take another look at *West Side Story*. Here is the song-type structure:

Act One

Prologue: Dance.

"Jet Song": Uptempo song.

"Something's Coming": Solo uptempo ballad, a "want song" in the formula.

"The Dance at the Gym": Dance.

"Maria": Solo ballad.

"Tonight": Duet, uptempo ballad.

"America": Comic song.

"Cool": Dance.

"One Hand, One Heart": Ballad, duet.

"Tonight Quintet": Canon.

"The Rumble": Fight in dance form.

Act Two

"I Feel Pretty": Tempo song.

"Somewhere": Ballad and dance.

"Gee, Officer Krupke": Comic song.

"A Boy Like That" and "I Have a Love": Fierce duet.

Notice how, in contrast to so many modern musicals, each sequence is in a different form than the ones around it.

Also notice in particular the application of form to each section. For the battle between the two camps: dance. For the love story: song. For the generation gap: dialogue. (Notice also that the four adults in the story—Doc, Lt. Shrank, Officer Krupke, and Gladhand—never sing or dance, and thus never really enter the world of the teenagers.)

Each plot point is essayed with the most appropriate form. Then the separate sequences are seamlessly melded.

Here are some of the most obvious categories, followed by examples from two classic musicals, *Kiss Me Kate* and *Pajama Game*:

	Kiss Me Kate	*The Pajama Game*
Opening Numbers	"Another Opening, Another Show"	"The Pajama Game" "Racing With the Clock"
"Want Songs"	"Why Can't You Behave" "Where Is the Life That Late I Lead?"	"A New Town Is a Blue Town"
Comedy Solos	"Always True to You (In My Fashion)"	"Think of the Time I Save"
Duets	"Brush Up Your Shakespeare"	"I'll Never Be Jealous Again"
Group Numbers	"We Open in Venice"	"Once a Year Day"
Love Songs	"Wunderbar" "So in Love" "Were Thine That Special Face"	"Small Talk"
Dance Numbers	"Too Darn Hot" "Tom, Dick, or Harry"	"Steam Heat"
The Hero's Manifesto	"I've Come to Wive It Wealthily in Padua"	"Hey There"
The Heroine's Manifesto	"I Hate Men"	"I'm Not at All in Love"
First Act Finales	"Kiss Me, Kate"	"There Once Was a Man"
Eleven O'Clock Numbers	"I Am Ashamed That Women Are So Simple"	"Hernando's Hideaway"
Finales	"Kiss Me Kate (reprise)"	"7 1/2 Cents"

Sure, you say, these are old-fashioned musicals. I don't want to write to formula, I want to write the new, post-modern musical. Here are both structures from Michael Bennett's *A Chorus Line* and *Dreamgirls*. First, the story structure.

The Hero's Journey	A Chorus Line	Dreamgirls
1. Ordinary World	The audition ("I Hope I Get It")	Three black girls, anxious to break into show business, begin with a talent contest.
2. Call to Adventure	Zach lines them up, asks them to introduce themselves.	They go professional, backing up a male star.
3. Refusal of the Call	Mike: "Don't you want to start at the end?"	
4. Meeting with the Mentor	Zach wants to know their stories.	They get signed by a manager.
5. Crossing the First Threshold	"I Can Do That"	They record a song. ("Cadillac Car") . . .
6. Tests, Allies, Enemies	"Hello Twelve, Hello Thirteen, Hello Love"	But are knocked off the charts by a white group.
7. Approach	"Dance: Ten; Looks: Three"	A hit requires payola ("Steppin' to the Bad Side") . . .
8. Ordeal	"One"	And firing the fat girl ("And I Am Tellin' You I'm Not Goin').
9. Reward	"The Tap Combination"	But the fat girl makes a comeback ("One Night Only").
10. The Road Back	"The Music and the Mirror"	The act breaks up . . .

The Hero's Journey	A Chorus Line	Dreamgirls
11. Resurrection	"What I Did for Love"	And goes their separate ways.
12. Return with Elixir	"One (reprise)"	The fat one gets back on top.

Now, the song type structure.

	A Chorus Line	Dreamgirls
Opening Numbers	"I Hope I Get It"	"Move (You're Steppin' on My Heart)"
"Want Songs"	"I Can Do That"	"Fake Your Way to the Top"
Comedy Solos, Duets, and Group Numbers	"Nothing" "Sing!" "Hello Twelve, Hello Thirteen, Hello Love"	"Ain't No Party"
Love Songs	"What I Did for Love"	"When I First Saw You"
Dance Numbers	"The Music and the Mirror"	"Steppin' to the Bad Side"
The Hero's Manifesto	Paul's monologue	"Family"
The Heroine's Manifesto	"At the Ballet" and "Dance: Ten; Looks: Three"	"Dreamgirls" and "I Am Changing"
First Act Finales	(no intermission)	"And I Am Telling You I'm Not Going"
Eleven O'Clock Numbers	"One" and "The Tap Combination"	"One Night Only"
Finales	"One"	"Hard to Say Goodbye My Love"

In summation, the book musical needs both a dramatic structure and a musical structure, and the two need to be allied.

The overall structure of a musical conforms to a timeless dramatic formula that goes back to Aristotle (in brief: "A whole is that which has a beginning, a middle, and an end"). The *interior structure of individual scenes* is the unique property of the American book musical. In order to keep the musical sequences within the range of believability they began to subscribe to, the golden age authors worked to structure their scenes and songs in a very fluid fashion, so that performers could stay in character throughout. Here are two examples of this technique. The book, music, and lyrics of each are wonderful, but they're set forth here because of the structure of the individual scenes. The interior structure of a song/scene requires finesse. Well-written, the song sneaks into the scene, which increases the seamlessness of the musical and the believability of the singing (or dancing). Sometimes the lyrics are woven around dialogue (or vice versa). Ideally, the dialogue is carrying the story, appropriate for the characters, and building to a musical number without being too obvious. Just like succeeding scenes in drama, the ideas behind the songs must seem an *inevitable outgrowth of the story* at that point. Bad examples, heard in two Broadway shows: "Bring on my court dancers!" and "Come on, baby, sing that song I like." Herewith, two excellent examples.

Fiorello! Book by Jerome Weidman, George Abbott; music by Jerry Bock; lyrics by Sheldon Harnick. Act One, Scene Two. Note how the lyrics to the song give us information; how the scene is woven into the song. Note also how the song grows out of simple poker talk to (1) include dialogue that moves the story forward and (2) proposes a nice metaphor, "Politics and Poker."

Five "Political Hacks" are playing poker around a green baize poker table. BEN is not in the game, he is pacing.

FIRST HACK: What do you say, Ben? You gonna take a hand?

BEN: Not now. Too much on my mind to play poker. Gotta settle on that damn candidate. (SEEDY MAN *enters*) Well, look who's here, my old friend Eddie Brown. How are you, Eddie?

SEEDY MAN: (*Correcting him*) No, Harry.

BEN: Sure, Harry, isn't that what I said? Here—(*Takes a dollar from the pot*)—vote Republican—carfare.

SEEDY MAN: You bet, Mr. Marino. You can count on me. (*He exits.*)

BEN: I doubt it.

THIRD HACK: That's your man, Ben. Run him.

BEN: May come to that yet. How about you? All you have to do—

THIRD HACK: I know, I know—

FIFTH HACK: He's done it twice.

THIRD HACK: Nothing doing. This time get yourself a brand-new sucker.

FIRST HACK. (*To* BEN) Sure you don't want to be dealt in?

BEN: No, go ahead.

(They sing)

FIRST HACK:
King bets.

SECOND HACK:
Cost you five.
Tony, up to you.

THIRD HACK:
I'm in.

FOURTH HACK:
So am I.

FIFTH HACK:
Likewise.

FIRST HACK:
Me too.

BEN: (*While the cards are being dealt*)
Gentlemen, here we are, and one thing is clear:
We gotta pick a candidate for Congress this year.

FIRST HACK:
Big ace.

SECOND HACK:
Ace bets.

THIRD HACK:
You'll pay—through the nose.

FOURTH HACK:
I'm in.

FIFTH HACK:
So am I.

FIRST HACK:
Likewise.

SECOND HACK:
Here goes.

FIRST HACK: *(Examining the hands)*
Possible straight,
Possible flush,
Nothing.

BEN:
Gentlemen, how about some names we can use?
Some qualified Republican who's willing to lose?

SECOND HACK:
How's about we should make Jack Riley the guy?

THIRD HACK:
Which Riley are you thinking of? Jack B. or Jack Y.?

BEN:
I say neither one,
I never even met 'em.

FOURTH HACK:
I say:
When you've got a pair of jacks,
Bet 'em!

ALL:
Politics and poker
Politics and poker
Shuffle up the cards
And find the joker.
Neither game's for children,
Either game is rough.
Decision, decisions, like:
Who to pick,
How to play,
What to bet,
When to call a bluff.

BEN: *(Speaking)* All right, now, fellas, politics or poker? Which is more important?

FIRST HACK: *(Singing)*
Pair of treys.

SECOND HACK:

Bet 'em.

THIRD HACK:

Little treys,
Good as gold.

FOURTH HACK:

I'll stay.

FIFTH HACK:

Raise you five.

FIRST HACK:

I'll call.

SECOND HACK:

I'll fold.

THIRD HACK:

Raise you back.

FOURTH HACK:

I think you're bluffin'.

THIRD HACK:

Put your money where your mouth is.

BEN:

Gentlemen, knock it off, and let's get this done.

FIFTH HACK:

Try Michael Paniaschenkowitz, I'm certain he'd run.

BEN.

Mike is out. I'm afraid he just wouldn't sell
Nobody likes a candidate whose name they can't spell.

FIRST HACK:

How about Dave Zimmerman?

BEN:

Davy's too bright.

SECOND HACK:

What about Walt Gustafson?

BEN:

Walt died last night.

THIRD HACK:

How about Frank Monahan?

FOURTH HACK:

What about George Gale?

BEN:

Frank ain't a citizen, and
George is in jail.

FIFTH HACK:

We could run Al Wallenstein.

BEN:

He's only twenty-three.

FIRST HACK:

What about Ed Peterson?

SECOND HACK:

You idiot! That's me!

ALL:

Politics and poker
Politics and poker
Playing for a pot
That's mediocre.
Politics and poker,
Running neck and neck.
If politics seems more
Predicable that's because usually you can stack the deck!

(*Enter* MARIE)

MARIE: Mr. Marino.

BEN: Well, if it isn't my old friend Miss Fischer. How are you, Miss Fischer?

MARIE: I came over because I want you to make the acquaintance of my boss, Mr. LaGuardia.

THIRD HACK: Huh!

BEN: Who?

THIRD HACK: That little wop with the big hat. *(Contemptuous)* Fiorello. You know him. He hangs around Silky Hetzel's in the Twelfth.

(FIORELLO *enters*)

FIORELLO: There are no little wops. Just big ones. And I'm ready and willing to demonstrate.

THIRD HACK: A modest guy, huh?

FIORELLO: No, just a guy who happens to believe the way to beat Tammany is not—*(Reaches over, takes the THIRD HACK'S cards, and tosses them to center of table)*—by throwing in your cards. I came over to get this nomination.

FIRST HACK: Is he kiddin'?

FIORELLO: I never kid about serious issues, and I'm sitting on one right now that's big enough and hot enough to elect a Congressman from this district.

MARIE: Ben, what have you got to lose?

BEN: *(Dry)* Just another election, that's all.

FIORELLO: You've been doing that long enough. Here's your chance to win for a change.

BEN: With what?

FIORELLO: The people of your own district. You think the men and women of the Fourteenth like the tenth-rate tinhorns they've had representing them in Congress for years?

BEN: And you think—?

FIORELLO: You give me the nomination, and I'll give you a Congressman.

BEN: And if you don't?

FIORELLO: *(Holds up his large sombrero)* See this hat?

BEN: You might get indigestion.

FIORELLO: I'll take my chances on that. Do I get the nomination?

BEN: *(Shrugging)* Why not?

MARIE: Congratulations, Mr. Marino, you've just got yourself a wonderful candidate.

FIORELLO: Call me tomorrow and I'll show you how to lay out the campaign. Right now, I've got to go take care of the hot issue that's going to help elect me. Come on, Marie.

(FIORELLO *and* MARIE *exit*)

BEN: *(Dry)* Well, we got that settled.

(The music starts. The players sing.)

THIRD HACK:
Gimme three.

FOURTH HACK:
Likewise.

FIFTH HACK:
None for me. Standing pat.

FIRST HACK.
Up to you.

SECOND HACK:
I'm in.

THIRD HACK:
I'm out.

FOURTH HACK:
I'm flat.

FIFTH HACK: (*Staring in direction taken by* FIORELLO)
Wonder why any guy would lead with his chin
Don't Fiorello realize he ain't gonna win?

SECOND HACK:
Ain't it obvious the
Odds are too great?

BEN:
Some guys
Always gotta try to fill an inside straight.

(*He speaks*)

If they didn't, where the hell would the fun be in the game?
(*He joins the game.*)

ALL:

Politics and poker.

Politics and poker

Makes the av'rage guy

A heavy smoker.

Bless the nominee,

And give him our regards,

And watch while he learns

that in poker and politics,

Brother you gotta have

that slippery hap-hazardous commodity

You gotta have the cards!

(Blackout)

The second example is *1776*, about which we've already discussed the uniqueness of the subject as a musical. Here I suspect the songwriter has written a terrific song, and it's up to the librettist to make it feel like it fits. Look for, "How did he win you, Madame?" which is a pretty bald setup, but at which the librettist arrives casually. Also the escalation to the simple dance, all in a metaphor—okay, a flat-out double entendre—that gives the song a second level, something that many good songs (such as, "I'm in Love With a Wonderful Guy") don't even have. She's in love with a wonderful guy, and that's it. But Thomas Jefferson, well, he "Plays the Violin."

We are on a street in Philadelphia. John Adams is pacing under Thomas Jefferson's window. Benjamin Franklin arrives.

FRANKLIN: Sorry to be late, John—I was up 'til all hours. Have y'been here long?

JOHN. Not long.

FRANKLIN: And what're y'doing out here? I expected you'd be up there cracking the whip.

JOHN: The shutters are still closed.

FRANKLIN: My word, so they are! Well, as the French say—

JOHN: Oh, *please*, Franklin! Spare me your bawdy mind first thing in the morning! *(They regard the closed shutters.)* Dare we call?

FRANKLIN: A Congressman dares anything. Go ahead.

JOHN: *Me?*

FRANKLIN: Your voice is more piercing.

JOHN: *(He starts, then hesitates.)* This is positively indecent!

FRANKLIN: Oh, John, they're young and they're in love.

JOHN: Not them, Franklin—us! Standing out here—*(He gestures vaguely at the shuttered room.)*—waiting for them to—I mean, what will people think?

FRANKLIN: Don't worry, John. The history books will clean it up.

JOHN: It doesn't matter. I won't appear in the history books, anyway—only you. (*He thinks about it.*) Franklin did this, Franklin did that, Franklin did some other damned thing. Franklin smote the ground, and out sprang George Washington, fully grown and on his horse. Franklin then electrified him with his miraculous lightning rod, and the three of them—Franklin, Washington, and the horse—conducted the entire Revolution all by themselves.

(*A pause*)

FRANKLIN: I like it!

(*Now the shutter opens and MARTHA appears, dressed and radiant. She is humming a tune.*)

FRANKLIN: Look at her, John—just look at her!

JOHN: (*Hypnotized.*) I am.

FRANKLIN: She's even more magnificent than I remember! Of course, we didn't see much of her front last night. (*Calling.*) Good morrow, madame! (*She looks down at him blankly.*)

JOHN: Good morrow!

MARTHA: Is it the habit in Philadelphia for strangers to shout at ladies from the street?

FRANKLIN: Not at all, Madame, but we're not—

MARTHA: And from men of your age it is not only unseemly, it's unsightly.

JOHN: Excuse me, madame, but we met last evening.

MARTHA: I spoke to no one last evening.

FRANKLIN: Indeed you did not, madame, but nevertheless we presented ourselves. This is Mr. John Adams and I am Dr. Franklin. *(As she stares at him, dumfounded)* Inventor of the stove?

MARTHA: Oh, please, I know your names very well. But you say you presented yourselves?

FRANKLIN *(Smiling)* It's of no matter. Your thoughts were well taken elsewhere.

MARTHA: *(Turning to the room for a moment)* My husband is not up yet.

FRANKLIN: Shall we start over? Please join us, madame.

MARTHA: Yes, of course. *(She disappears from the window.)*

FRANKLIN: No wonder the man couldn't write. Who could think of independence, married to her?

(She appears, smiling.)

MARTHA: I beg you to forgive me. It is indeed an honor meeting the two greatest men in America.

FRANKLIN: *(Smiling back)* Certainly the greatest within earshot, anyway.

MARTHA: I am not an idle flatterer, Dr. Franklin. My husband admires you both greatly.

FRANKLIN: Then we are doubly flattered, for we admire very much that which your husband admires.

(A pause as they regard each other warmly. They have hit it off.)

JOHN: *(Finally; the bull in the china shop)* Did you sleep well, madame? *(FRANKLIN nudges him with his elbow.)* I mean, did you lie comfortably? Oh, damn! Y'know what I mean!

FRANKLIN: Yes, John, we do. Tell us about yourself, madame; we've had precious little information. What's your first name?

MARTHA: Martha.

FRANKLIN: Ah, Martha. He might at least have told us that. I'm afraid your husband doesn't say very much.

JOHN: He's the most silent man in Congress. I've never heard him utter three sentences together.

FRANKLIN: Not everyone's a talker, John.

MARTHA: It's true, you know. *(She turns to look at the window.)* Tom is not—a talker.

(She sings.)

Oh, he never speaks his passions,
He never speaks his views.
Whereas other men speak volumes,
The man I love is mute.

In truth
I can't recall
Being woo'd with words
At all.

Even now . . . .

(Music continues under)

JOHN: *(Speaking)* Go on, madame.

FRANKLIN: How did he win you, Martha, and how does he hold onto a bounty such as you?

MARTHA: Surely you've noticed that Tom is a man of many accomplishments; author, lawyer, farmer, architect, statesman— *(She hesitates.)*—and still one more that I hesitate to mention.

JOHN: Don't hesitate, madame—don't hesitate!

FRANKLIN: Yes, what *else* can that redheaded tombstone do?

MARTHA: *(She looks at them for a moment, then leans in and sings, confidentially.)*
He plays the violin

He tucks it right under his chin,
And he bows,
Oh, he bows,
For he knows,
Yes, he knows, that it's . . .

Heigh, heigh, heigh diddle-diddle,
'Twixt my heart, Tom, and his fiddle,
My strings are unstrung.
Heigh-heigh-heigh-heigh-igh-igh . . .
Heigh! I am undone!

(JOHN *and* FRANKLIN *look at one another, not at all sure if she's putting them on or not.*)

FRANKLIN: *(Speaking)* The violin, madame?

MARTHA:
I hear his violin
and I get that feeling within,
And I sigh . . .
Oh, I sigh . . .
He draws near,
Very near, and it's . . .

Heigh, heigh, heigh diddle-diddle, and . . .
Good-by to the fiddle!
My strings are unstrung.
Heigh-heigh-heigh-heigh-igh-igh . . .
Heigh—I'm always undone!

FRANKLIN: *(Speaking)* That settles it, John, we're taking up the violin!

JOHN: *(To Martha)* Very well, madame, you've got us playing the violin! What happens next?

MARTHA: Why, just what you'd expect.

(JOHN *and* FRANKLIN *exchange expectant looks.*)

MARTHA: We dance!

JOHN and FRANKLIN *(Together and to each other)* Dance?

FRANKLIN: Incredible!

MARTHA: One-two-three, one-two-three!

(And in an instant she has swept FRANKLIN off into an energetic waltz. JOHN watches them for a moment, still trying to understand.)

JOHN: Who's playing the violin?

FRANKLIN: Oh, John—really!

(And MARTHA leaves FRANKLIN to begin waltzing with JOHN, who, to FRANKLIN'S astonishment, turns out to dance expertly.)

FRANKLIN: John! You can dance!

JOHN: (*Executing an intricate step—he is having a grand time.*) We still do a few things in Boston, Franklin! (*Finally they have twirled and spun and danced themselves out.*)

MARTHA: (*Singing, as she catches her breath*)
When Heaven calls to me,
Sing me no sad elegy!
Say I died
Loving bride,
Loving wife,
Loving life. Oh, it was . . .

MARTHA, JOHN, and FRANKLIN:
Heigh, heigh, heigh diddle-diddle . . .

MARTHA:
'Twixt my heart, Tom, and his
Fiddle, and
Ever 'twill be
Heigh-heigh-heigh-heigh-igh-igh . . .
Heigh, through eternity.

FRANKLIN (*In counterpoint*)
He plays the violin . . .

JOHN: (*In counterpoint*)
He plays the violin . . .

MARTHA (*In counterpoint*)
He plays the violin!

(They bow to her, and she curtsies. Now JEFFERSON *appears, a fiddle under his arm, and stuck on the end of his bow is a paper. He collects his wife, and together they start back toward the room.)*

JOHN: Franklin, look! He's written something—he's done it! *(He dashes after them, snatches the paper off the bow, and comes back to* FRANKLIN, *delighted, and reads it.)* "Dear Mr. Adams: I am taking my wife back to bed. Kindly go away. Y'r ob'dt, T. Jefferson."

FRANKLIN: What, again?

JOHN: Incredible.

FRANKLIN: Perhaps I'm the one who should've written the declaration, after all. At my age there's little doubt that the pen is mightier than the sword.

(He sings.)

For it's
Heigh, heigh, heigh diddle-diddle

(Enviously)

And god bless the man who can fiddle . . .

JOHN: *(Ever the old warhorse)*
And independency!

JOHN and FRANKLIN: *(Regaining their energy)*

Heigh-heigh-heigh-heigh-igh-igh

Yata-ta-ta-tah!

Through eternity!

(And they exit arm in arm.)

He plays the violin! . . . Violin! . . . Violin!

These, then, are the basic rules of the book musical: (1) That the musical sequences grow out of the strongest emotional ideas of the story. (2) That the songs vary in type, (3) the music is authentic to the time and place, and (4) the lyrics express the character(s) singing them. (5) That the dances move the story forward, and (6) express the character's feelings. (7) That the songs are (roughly) evenly spaced, (8) without crippling a strong dramatic structure. (9) And finally, that you don't have to follow these rules. Musical entertainment can take many and varied forms. Nevertheless, a number of great American book musicals adhered to these rules to their advantage.

A minor structural issue that needs addressing is reprises. Those that serve the composer's desire to pound a melody into the audience's ear so that they'll rush out to buy the sheet music only serve to slow a second act down. (George Kaufman to Frank Loesser during rehearsals for *Guys and Dolls*: "If you reprise your songs, I'll reprise my jokes.") Those that serve to build a *new idea* upon an old one can work wonders, for the audience already knows the melody, and now only has to assimilate the new lyrics. This, then, comes in the category of having your cake (the composer's) and eating it too. An effective reprise must add some sort of twist or irony to the original idea, not just remind us of the original idea.

Example: "Agony" from *Into the Woods*. In Act I, two princes sing of their love (lust?) for Cinderella and Rapunzel. In Act II, having achieved their desire, they reprise the song over different girls! The reprise emphasizes how fickle a prince can be, and surprises us with a (comic) change in direction of their libidos.

Second example: "You're Lovely": two duets from *A Funny Thing Happened on the Way to the Forum*. Act One, Hero sings it about Philia, who sings it about herself. Act Two, with Hysterium in drag, Pseudolus sings it about him, and Hysterium sings it about himself!

Final example, from an earlier era, is the use of the Gershwin's "Who Cares" ("Who cares what the public chatters/Love's the only thing that matters"). It's first sung "brightly, even glibly" in a lighthearted way. Later, when the lead, Wintergreen, is told he must give up his wife for political considerations, he sings it slowly, on a dark stage, and it was moving and romantic.

Finally, important to the structure of any linear drama is the premise, the setup, the conceit. Superman is a believable character *because he's from the planet Krypton, where the gravity is denser.* If we didn't know that, we simply couldn't buy his super powers. It has to be said, and it has to be said up front. (Since everyone in the civilized world knows this by now, it no longer needs explanation in every succeeding issue or sequel. But it's there.) A musical's version of the premise is the opening number.

CHAPTER 6

Another Opening, Another Show

"I can tell about a musical in the first twenty minutes."
—David Merrick

The most significant legend regarding opening numbers is the one in which Robbins, doctoring *A Funny Thing Happened on the Way to the Forum*, nixed the original opening (and charming song) "Love Is in the Air," in favor of "Comedy Tonight," which Sondheim wrote at Robbins request during tryouts. Robbins said, in effect, you've got to begin by telling the audience what they are about to see, and *Forum's* genre was farce, not romance. In one of the great turnarounds in musical theatre history, that one song caused the audience to laugh at the rest of the show, something they hadn't been doing, to the frantic consternation of the creators. The new opening told the audience it was okay to laugh, and they did.

Opening numbers were Robbins' forté. The exuberance with which sailors blast out of their ship and onto the streets of New York for their twenty-four hours of R and R in *On the Town* ("New York, New York"), the escalating battle for the streets between whites and Puerto Ricans in *West Side Story* ("Prologue"), the detailing of what "Tradition" means as the entire village is introduced in

Fiddler on the Roof, and the hysterical, burlesque, and vaudeville staging of the company about to present a "Comedy Tonight" in *Forum* were all his achievements. (And, of course, those of the authors.) And don't forget Ethel Merman charging down the aisle, dog under arm, shouting, "Sing out, Louise!"

Robbins was well known for constantly demanding of the authors he worked with, *"What is this show about?"* Besides keeping the rewrites on track—often a hectic and constant process during out-of-town tryouts—the answer to this question almost always led to an outstanding opening number.

When, during its evolution, *Pippin* developed a framework in which a troupe of players, led by a Leading Player, were putting on a show, Stephen Schwartz wrote "Magic to Do" ("just for you . . . ") for the opening. From there designer Tony Walton invented the curtain of light and fog, out of which stepped Fosse's slick cast. It was quite breathtaking.

Introducing all the characters and their own stories is often effective. *1776* combines three themes: the weather and location ("It's hot as hell in Philadelphia" "Someone ought to open up a window . . . No, no, no, too many flies"), which explains the crankiness of all the delegates; John Adams' stubborn fight for a declaration of independence by the colonies and the fierce opposition to it ("And by God I have had this Congress . . . "); and his loneliness (via sung letters between he and his wife Abigail).

There's nothing like a rousing, full company opening sequence. On the other hand . . .

Let's not forget that Hammerstein's discovery with *Oklahoma!*—an older woman is churning butter, a cowboy strolls on singing— is also effective in *My Fair Lady*: Higgins overhears Eliza and explains that the English butcher their own language. Both are in the "let's-get-the-plot-started" category. Bring on the girls if you can, but more important, start giving the audience not just entertainment, but *information*.

That, I suppose, is the key. We can't be too narrow about a good opening. What definition could contain all the above examples? And it's outside the purview of these theories to try and explain what's entertaining and what isn't. (You'll know it when you see it.) But we can say that an opening number needs to do one or more of several things: establish style. Set the tone for the evening. State the premise. Introduce the principal characters and their needs. Introduce time and place. (And if you can do all that in one number, you're a better man than I, Gunga Din.)

Talking to the audience, or some variation of it (Tevye's God, Dolly to deceased husband, or *A Chorus Line*'s director) is a useful technique, recently effective in *The Light in the Piazza*. It gives the author an additional avenue for passing information that might be awkward exposition otherwise ("In our little village of Anatevka . . . "). It gives the audience a direct connection with the characters and circumstances, makes them feel *included*. I list this technique here, because if a character is going to talk to us directly, that's a unique style, and has to be introduced with the premise.

Neil Simon employed this technique very effectively in *Promises, Promises*. The film it was based on did not feature the musical's sequences in which Chuck Baxter halts the onstage proceedings to say a few words to the audience. The show, however, begins with:

CHUCK BAXTER is at his desk working at an adding machine. He looks up and notices the audience.

CHUCK: The main problem with working as a hundred-and-twelve-dollar-a-week accountant in a seventy-two story insurance company with assets of over three billion dollars that employs thirty-one thousand two hundred and fifty-nine people here in the New York office alone . . . is that it makes a person feel so God-awful *puny.* (*He resumes work, then stops.*) Not that I don't have aspirations and ambitions. I definitely have aspirations and ambitions . . . As you can see it's five-forty and everyone else went home at five-thirty and I didn't go home at five-thirty because Mr. Sheldrake, the personnel manager, doesn't leave until five-forty and I thought it wouldn't hurt, promotion-wise, if he saw me working past five-thirty. (SHELDRAKE *enters, heading for the elevators; he rings the elevator bell.*) Evening, Mr. Sheldrake . . . How are you, Mr. Sheldrake . . . You're looking well, Mr. Sheldrake . . . (SHELDRAKE *enters the elevator.*) Nice seeing you again, Mr. Sheldrake. Good-by, Mr. Sheldrake. (SHELDRAKE *has gone. Crossing in front of the desk, CHUCK sits against it.*) If you've noticed, I'm the kind of person that people don't notice . . . I wish I were sitting out there with you so I could take a look at me and figure out what's wrong.

At which point, he sings "Half as Big As Life," a hero's lament, or "want song," if ever there was one. Then:

(*He crosses behind the desk and puts on his jacket.*) Not that there aren't some people around here who've noticed I'm something more than a nine-to-five adding machine . . . Like this real pretty girl who works up in the Employees' Cafeteria, Fran Kubelik . . . *she* notices . . . Oh, Miss Kubelik . . . Working late too, I see.

FRAN: Oh, hello, Chuck. Yes, I had a few things to take care of in the cafeteria and I thought I'd just—Oh, what's the use, Chuck. I stayed late because I wanted to see you. I guess it's no secret that I'm enormously attracted to you but you never seem to pay any attention to me . . . Look, Chuck, can't we go somewhere and have a drink because—

CHUCK (*Raises his hand*): Wait! Hold it a second! (FRAN freezes, CHUCK turns to the audience.) It's not true. She never said that. I mean, I can kid myself but there's no point in lying to you. I'm not doing too well in this department either. So sometimes I dream up conversations . . . (*He looks at her, then back to the audience.e*) Well, you can hardly blame me, can you? . . . No, what she actually said was—

FRAN: Oh, hello, how are you, Frank?

CHUCK: Chuck! Chuck Baxter.

FRAN: Oh yes, I'm sorry.

CHUCK: That's all right. How are things in the cafeteria?

FRAN: Fine. I didn't see you there last week. Were you sick?

CHUCK: No, I was there. You just didn't see me . . . Look, if you're not in a hurry to get home, I was wondering if—

FRAN: Oh, excuse me, Chuck, I'm in a hurry to get home. Bye. (*She exits into the elevator*)

No big opening number, just the leading man talking to us, establishing his character, singing a song that defines his character ("Half as big as life, that's me . . . ") and hopes ("I've got lots of dreams . . . "). He will eventually have a lot more to do with Fran. As in *Oklahoma!*, where Hammerstein bucked tradition by passing up a big opening number in favor of Curly singing "Oh, What a Beautiful Morning," *Promises* does the same to great effect. And while there's nothing wrong with splashy opening numbers to perk up an audience, *Oklahoma!* and *Promises* feature an opening just as good: introduce the main character and start the story.

Man of La Mancha also opens with the introduction of the hero. The first powerful image that garners our attention here is Howard Bay's set. The staircase lowers and the guards bring Cervantes down into a foreboding gloom. Next comes the transformation of the man, Miguel de Cervantes, into the hero of his novel, Don Quixote. Attempting to pacify the growling inmates of the prison, Cervantes offers to tell them a story ("I shall impersonate a man . . . "). The sequence builds until Cervantes is Quixote, astride his gallant steed Rocinante, exclaiming, "I am I, Don Quixote, the lord of La Mancha . . . "

42nd Street opens on tapping feet. And no more, for the curtain, rising up to their knees, stops, and lets us watch a herd of pounding feet for a moment, before it rises the rest of the way. (This is a nod to the producer Max Gordon, who said, "I can tell about a musical before the curtain is halfway up," referring to the legs of the chorines.) It's a clever bit, because it tells you what kind of show you are about to see—tap and more tap.

Champion, however, had done more complicated openings, some in the breathtaking category. His most famous was *Carnival.* Starting on an utterly bare stage with only the sky and a lone tree to set the place, his cast erected an entire carnival, singing "Direct From Vienna" to announce themselves.

One caveat. The opening number in *Bye Bye Birdie* is *not* "The Telephone Hour." (Gotcha!) In fact, *Birdie* opens on a small scene between Albert, the manager of a rock singer who is about to be drafted and leave him unemployed, and his girlfriend, who would like to get married, but to a secure "English Teacher," not an unemployed music manager. First song: a solo for the girlfriend. This might seem to be a problem on paper. It works, however, and we might credit George Abbott's famous dictum: "Better to start slow than end slow." *Birdie builds* to "The Telephone Hour." That might make today's producers a little nervous, but, not unlike sex, the longer the foreplay, the better the climax.

Bennett, another expert at openings, starts *Dreamgirls* with four singers performing "onstage." Surprise, they're not the girls whose story we're about to see; they're just another group we won't hear from again. Two things: first, Bennett is setting up a story about show business ("It's showbiz, just showbiz . . . "), and here it is, at the beginning, an amateur contest. (When it ends with a star-filled reunion, we've traveled the entertainment business from bottom to top.) Second, before the opening sequence is over, we have met all the girls we *are* going to follow, as well as the men around them.

Carousel begins with a unique sequence, a pantomime to Rodger's original musical theme that introduces our anti-hero. He gets fired for flirting with the girls riding his carousel.

Some musicals begin not with the main characters, or the story, but with the framework. *A Chorus Line* opens on the auditions, and "I Hope I Get It" rapidly discloses the desperate passions of the dancers looking for a job. The story in *Chorus Line* isn't really the audition, it's the lives of the dancers, but the audition provides the milieu, the framework. In the end, we'll see who gets the job, and the two themes will dovetail, for our empathy with each dancer will be met or not as we hear the director tick off who is hired and who isn't.

The great showbiz anthem, "There's No Business Like Show Business" pops up in the middle of the first act of *Annie Get Your Gun*, beautifully positioned as a "book" number, because the cast of Buffalo Bill's Wild West Show explains this maxim to the newcomer. Thinking it the most popular and best song in the show, Peter Stone, authoring a revised version, placed it as an opening number. Great song all right, but now not as effective within the book for the fact that it's now a reprise. Stone's new framework—a show-within-a-show—suggested this, but all in all, the politically correct rewrite did little to help the classic musical.

(Don't ask me how *Annie* gets away with the plaintive ballad "Maybe" by the kid, followed by the tuneful but boringly staged, "It's the Hard-Knock Life" by the orphans. I can only guess that the audience just loves tots.)

In the end, we might divide successful openings into two categories. Either they introduce the main characters—*Damn Yankees, How to Succeed in Business Without Really Trying, Man of La Mancha, My Fair Lady*—or they introduce the milieu—*Fiddler on the Roof* ("Tradition"), *Follies, A Funny Thing Happened on the Way to the Forum* ("Comedy Tonight"), *Guys and Dolls* ("Runyonland" and "Fugue for Tinhorns"), *The Music Man* ("Rock Island" and "Iowa Stubborn"), *The Pajama Game* ("The pajama game is the game we love . . . "). Introducing both can be doubly effective (*1776, Dreamgirls, Gypsy*).

Part of the lore of the BMI Musical Theater Writer's Workshop is that you must write your opening number last. The thought behind this is that you must know what your show is all about before you can fix on the subject of the opening, and until you've written the body of the show, you might not have a firm grasp on the theme. True, to a point. But if you don't have too much of a grasp on the overall concept, theme, and story of your musical, you probably shouldn't be writing anything at all yet. Nevertheless, whether you write your socko opening first, last, or somewhere in the middle of the long, frustrating, and angst-written process of creating a musical, this much is true: know what you're about to present, and write an opening that spells it out. You can choose from introducing the main characters, time and place, or style. Better yet, try to work in all three.

So you've got all your ducks in a row. You've got a great score. What you need next is great staging.

CHAPTER 7

The Choreographers Who Created the Golden Age

"Dance is the hidden language of the soul."
—Martha Graham

Before 1943, dancing in musicals was primarily tap and kick lines, often so generic that various routines could be inserted in various shows willy-nilly with ill effect. Ballets were self-contained, unrelated to the story, and in the classical Russian style. Dancers participated in uptempo songs without dramatic logic. But in the 1930s, a radical revolution began in all the arts. Creative writers, painters, composers, and choreographers were working to expand the boundaries of the classical arts, to express deeper, more profound feelings, and to express the American character in a new, American vernacular.

With all due respect to other outstanding choreographers, the following seven men and one woman were among them responsible for the rapid development of the new musical staging, and a new choreographic vocabulary for American theatre dance. Each of these eight choreographers used dance in new and dramatic ways, all but Alton and de Mille becoming successful directors as well, with the result that show after show benefited from the integration of movement and dance until song, dance, and scene became seamless. They are listed here by order of their first significant show, to their last original Broadway production.

Robert Alton (1933–1955)
Jack Cole (1943–1965)
Agnes de Mille (1943–1969)
Jerome Robbins (1944–1964)
Michael Kidd (1947–1993)
Gower Champion (1948–1980)
Bob Fosse (1954–1986)
Michael Bennett (1966–1981)

Robert Alton

After ballet training, the Vermont-born Alton began as a Broadway chorus boy in 1919, danced for the Mordkin Ballet (predecessor to American Ballet Theatre), and moved up in the ranks by assisting other choreographers. Alton first choreographed the Broadway musical *Hold Your Horses* in 1933 (ballets by Harriet Hoctor), which ran only 88 performances, and seems to have been a mishmash of material.

Although his stage choreography is lost to us, he was even more popular among Hollywood producers, and was the choreographer (and before that the "dance director," as early choreographers were billed) on the musical films *Broadway Rhythm*, *The Harvey Girls*, *Ziegfeld Follies*, *Till the Clouds Roll By*, *The Pirate*, *Easter Parade*, *Words and Music*, *The Barkleys of Broadway*, *In the Good Old Summertime*, *Annie Get Your Gun*, *Show Boat*, *The Belle of New*

York, Call Me Madam, White Christmas, There's No Business Like Show Business, and many others, all still popular with film musical fans for their wonderful musical numbers. The choreography in these films usually represents the best of the "presentational" approach: numbers that were presented directly to the audience, or, in this case, to the camera. (Which, in those days, didn't move so much or edit so much that the actual choreography was indecipherable.) Yet some of those films also feature innovative numbers already attempting to expand the thirty-two-bars-with-dance-interlude format. Many of them also feature great dancers: Fred Astaire in *The Belle of New York, The Barkleys of Broadway, Easter Parade, Ziegfeld Follies*, the Nicholas Brothers in *The Pirate*, Marge and Gower Champion in *Show Boat*, and Ray Bolger in *The Harvey Girls*. Clearly, Alton knew how to set up a star dancer, whether he provided the choreography or just helped.

Alton's vast body of work almost all falls into the category of pure show dancing, with little expression of character or plot. His vocabulary, however, is probably what made him the most sought-after choreographer of the period, and what brings him to our attention. Relying less on ballet than tap and jazz, and more on the burgeoning jazz music than operetta, he forged a vocabulary that was soon to evolve into American jazz dancing.

It was Alton's 1940 stage job, *Pal Joey*, that gives him first place on our list. As described to me by a dancer who saw the original Broadway production, the *Joey* chorus consisted of girls of many shapes and sizes, the most memorable of whom was a short girl clearly chewing gum during her numbers. As *Joey* is set in a downscale nightclub, this bit of realism was one of the first to break the habit of hiring beautiful, long-legged chorus girls in every production, no matter the setting, and instead attempt to create the appropriate ambiance for the story.

Jack Cole

As a teacher, dancer, and choreographer Cole's influence was wider, if less public, than any choreographer of the twentieth century. Though he is well known in dance circles as the father of jazz dance, today little remains of his direct legacy, outside of a number of B movies and the memory of those who saw his incendiary nightclub work and dances for Broadway musicals. His indirect legacy, however, is astoundingly pervasive.

Cole dancers who have seen Jerome Robbins' *Opus Jazz* and *West Side Story* swear to the Cole influence. Bob Fosse's muse was Gwen Verdon, a Cole-trained dancer. Ron Field, who created the dazzling musical staging for *Cabaret* and *Zorba* and directed and choreographed the slick Lauren Bacall vehicle *Applause*, was a Cole dancer, as were Ron Lewis, a principal architect of jazz dancing in Las Vegas shows and Carol Haney, a star dancer and choreographer.

Cole was the most experimental of all the dancer-choreographers of his era, eschewing the pure forms of classic ballet and modern dance and the tap and kick of early Broadway for an exotic amalgam influenced by them all, to which he added East Indian and African dances and the social dances of the twenties.

To begin with, he created the idea of hard work. Of physically rising to a level you would, as a dancer, never have thought possible.

Prior to Cole, dancers—you can see it in old black and white films—were graceful and athletic. Certainly before Actor's Equity, dancers rehearsed long hours for no pay. There may have been the Julian Marshes of *42nd Street*. ("You're going to work and sweat and work some more. You're going to work days, and you're going to work nights, and you're going to work between times. When I think you need it, you're going to dance until your feet fall off and you aren't able to stand up. But six weeks from now, we're going to have a SHOW!") But the truth is, the routines were not difficult, class was standard, and there was little striving for perfection. Cole's classes were brutal, his rehearsals worse, his demands enormous. A repetitive theme among all the dancers who speak about Cole is the brutally hard work. Cole created a coterie of favorite dancers he used for much of his work, but when he didn't have access to them—if he staged a show in London, or needed a larger number of dancers for a club act, film, or Broadway show—he would hold class, desperately working to train new dancers in his technique, often to the detriment of his choreography, which he sometimes left incomplete having run out of time.

By combining ballet and modern with both the ethnic dance he researched—East Indian and South American in particular—and folk dances from the world over, and adding to that the social dances of the jazz era—the Shimmy, Black Bottom, Charleston, Camel Walk, and Lindy Hop—Cole evolved a vocabulary that has subsequently been titled "jazz dance." (In fact it was his friend Marcus Blechman's introduction of jazz music records to Cole that caused him to unite his dance vocabulary to the growing American musical form.)

This new vocabulary required *isolation* of the various body parts—individual parts of the body moving in contrast to, as opposed to in harmony with, other parts. He freed the pelvis. Outside of burlesque, this was just not done. He lowered a jazz dancer's center of gravity with deeper pliés. He turned *in* the feet. His dancers moved in unique ways they never had before, strengthening muscles they never knew they had.

It was his *terre á terre* style that really forced dancers to build strength. Cole used the *plié*—bent knees, low center of gravity—consistently in his work. Moreover, he was constantly diving into the ground—knee slides were one of his personal favorites—and then leaping into the air in great jumps. All this created the infamous "thunder thighs" of strong dancers, who became coiled springs.

In later years a dancer, doing a comic imitation of Bob Fosse, urged that an eyebrow move a quarter-inch higher during a step. This minute perfectionism could be traced to the Cole Technique. Cole was every bit as precise as that in his demands.

In fact, there was a remarkable Cult of Cole around the magnetic personality. Descriptions of Cole in class and rehearsal include his impatience; his explosive, mercurial temper; his sudden rages; his biting sarcasm; and his uncanny ability to sense a dancers' vulnerabilities. He once tried to throw a girl out of a second-story window, and when he really got angry, he could become absolutely deranged. To call Cole a taskmaster or a perfectionist stops well short of the effort he insisted upon from his dancers, as he cursed, swore, and used pornographic language in an attempt to create his sometimes erotic, always energetic, choreography.

His temper wasn't confined to the rehearsal room. On one occasion he stopped in the middle of performing his club act, turned to the conductor, and said, "You have your way of count-ing, and I have mine. Why don't we have a conference and see if we can't come to some sort of an agreement? Then we can get on with this show!" On another he simply took the baton out of the conductor's hand, and broke it over his knee.

If he was cruel to dancers, from whom he expected the highest standards, he was understanding and patient with actors and singers with two left feet. He loved making the stars of stage and screen look good in spite of their lack of ability, and counted among his loyal fans Alfred Drake, Jane Russell, Marilyn Monroe, Rita Hayworth, Betty Grable, Lana Turner, and Dolores Gray, many of whom requested him on their films and for their nightclub acts.

Cole's childhood portends his adult angst, for he was as hard on himself as he was on his dancers. A wandering eye made him shy and self-conscious. (An operation corrected it in adulthood, but he never lost a self-consciousness over his face, concentrating instead on his body.) He was boarded at a convent school and a military academy, and felt unloved by his mother and stepfather.

His background and his ability to survive on three hours of sleep created a tremendous fund of energy and determination on which he drove himself and his dancers to heights undreamed of previously. It came to be called the Cole Technique.

Cole's early training was with Ruth St. Denis and Ted Shawn (known in concert as Denishawn), and with Doris Humphrey and Charles Weidman (known as the Humphrey-Weidman dancers), all pioneers of modern dance. His fierce energy and magnetic personality in performance soon led to multiple engagements. On the road with Denishawn meant one-night stands and sleeping on buses for hardly any money, all for an art form not yet very popular in America. By contrast, the Humphrey-Weidman dancers performed a ballet in a Theatre Guild production of Moliere's *School for Husbands* that ran on Broadway for fifteen weeks, considerable in 1933, the depths of the Depression; and simultaneously booked the Palais Royale supper club, where Cole and a partner danced a steamy tango both before and after they ran to the theatre for *School for Husbands.*

Both during and subsequent to his career, dance purists would wonder why Cole, who was fiercely devoted to his art and always pushing the boundaries of dance, would nevertheless seldom appear in concert work, never begin the concert company that he sometimes mused about, but instead accepted gig after gig in supper clubs, films, and Broadway musicals. Clearly he enjoyed the financial remunerations. (When his agent quoted a price of $7,500 per week, the mobster that owned one club countered, "Tell him he gets $6,500 or he dances from now on in a cement kimono." Either way, that was a lot of money in the thirties.) But for someone as iconoclastic as Cole, there has to be something more. Perhaps it was the acceptance he hadn't had in childhood, for while modern dance companies were struggling to gain recognition, the Jack Cole dancers, usually featuring Jack Cole, became regulars at the Rainbow Room, the Copa, Slapsie Maxie's, the Latin Quarter, Chez Paree, Ciro's, Casa Mañana, and others in New York, Chicago, Florida, and Los Angeles. His satyric, dazzling, nearly violent personal style and the erotic jazz work and costumes of his girls made him hugely popular with the jaded drinking and smoking crowd, and the gangsters who owned the clubs. Contemporary observers claim that it was there he did his most innovative work. And though one biographer called Cole's nightclub work "pearls before swine," with titles like *Reefer Madness!*, *Blue Prelude*, *Minnie the Moocher*, and *Wedding of a Solid Sender*, it is clear why he was a hit on the supper club circuit. Unwilling to suffer the poverty associated with concert work, Cole simply took his dances to the supper clubs and Broadway revues, yet never compromised his work.

In 1941 he had an opportunity that would make any choreographer jealous. Harry Cohn at Columbia Pictures financed a permanent group of dancers on the lot, under Cole, so that they would always be ready for assignments in Cole-choreographed film musicals. It was an intense but greatly satisfying opportunity to have a home base, excellent financing, and the chance to work daily on technique, as well as preparing numbers for Columbia films. If Columbia wasn't MGM, and Cole's group was not part of the Freed Unit that produced so many classic film musicals, nevertheless his dances often saved otherwise boring pictures. Beginning with *Moon Over Miami* (in which his "Seminole Dance" was so erotic it was cut by the Hays Office Production Code) and extending through *Eadie Was a Lady*, *Kismet* (which he had staged on Broadway), *Gilda*, *Gentlemen Prefer Blondes*, *There's No Business Like Show Business*, *Les Girls*, *Some Like It Hot*, *Let's Make Love*, and numerous other films over three decades—at Columbia and later at Fox—Cole and his dancers created number after number. In many cases, today his dances are the high points of these B-movie musicals.

In spite of his propensity for walking off projects and having raging arguments with producers, Cole's output was enormous. In addition to constant night club work and the many films, he choreographed the Broadway musicals *Man of La Mancha*,

Foxy, A Funny Thing Happened on the Way to the Forum, Kean, Donnybrook!, Jamaica, Kismet, Alive and Kicking, Magdalena, Allah Be Praised! and *Something for the Boys.* If that list runs the gamut from classic to flop (it is with *Allah Be Praised!* that the famous story emerges in which the producer, Alfred Bloomingdale of the department store, was advised by an acquaintance to "close the show and keep the store open nights"), nevertheless, in almost every case critics and writers singled out his work as a highlight.

Buzz Miller, a Cole disciple and one of the most famous of Broadway dancers of his generation, thinks that the problem with today's dancers is to "get them wound up enough. To bring them to that pitch of excitement and preparedness where they can do the dance expertly." Broadway, however, still boasts the greatest jazz dancers in the world, and it was Cole who created them. From the X-rated needlepoint that relaxed him to the daily personal workouts he couldn't live without, to his teaching at UCLA, which formed the final epoch of his career and continued even while he hid the fact that he was dying, Cole was a hurricane force in the dance world. Though he did some directing, he was never really comfortable in command of entire shows, and for that reason, never became one of the celebrity super-directors.

Cole made no impression on the developing idea of integrated musical staging, being a pure dancer-choreographer who seldom directed. His research on ethnic and folk dances and his subsequent choreography, however, did have an effect on many of the generations of dancers who worked for him, and went on to careers of their own. Besides the Arabian Nights milieu he loved (*Kismet*), his influence sexualized Broadway choreography. His most famous dancer was Gwen Verdon, who influenced Bob Fosse. His staging of "The House of Marcus Lycus" in *A Funny Thing Happened on the Way to the Forum* consists of half a dozen courtesans, each displaying their "talents" in a unique solo.

Many of the choreographers of the golden age were demanding personalities, to say the least. So many were caustic slave drivers, one has to wonder about the sadomasochistic relationship between dancers and choreographers. Indeed, dancers almost have to be masochists to achieve technique, and sadism seems a natural progression as they get older and prepare to take the place of their choreographers and teachers.

Yet intensely hard work is the key to success. Musical theatre performers need a good deal of repetition, *until the technique becomes secondary to the emotions expressed.* The experience that allows well-trained performers to work quickly can be misleading, for until the flow of staging and choreography becomes second nature, the performer will not appear to be anything but an automaton. Only when the technical details—the dialogue, the notes, the movement, the choreography—are absorbed can the actor, singer, or dancer go beyond technique to presenting a believable character. A director-choreographer must therefore stage a musical quickly, leaving as much time as possible for the repetition that will allow the cast to subsume the technique.

Reaching an off-book run-through early in the rehearsal period is especially necessary for original productions, since there is no perfect way of knowing just how strong the overall structure is without seeing it on its feet. Hurriedly blocking scenes and songs, however, sometimes upsets those actors who, used to plays, want to work more slowly into the skin of the character and the fabric of the play before committing to "blocking." This dichotomy can create a tension for which the director must somehow compensate. The work ethic Cole introduced has had a profound effect on the Broadway musical.

In the end, friends arranged for Cole to enter the Motion Picture and Television Memorial Hospital, the industry's pasture. When he died, his students at UCLA sent his obituary to the *Los Angeles Times*, but they didn't bother printing it. His legacy, however, is burned into all the subsequent versions of theatre and jazz dance in American history.

Agnes de Mille

"By synthesizing the brilliance of classical ballet technique, the freedom of modern dance, and the familiarity of folk dances, [de Mille] created an original kind of movement that told a story in a theatrically striking way . . . " —Carol Easton, *No Intermissions*

It is quite amazing that de Mille, growing up in Beverly Hills as the daughter and niece of two of the most famous and successful men in early Hollywood—her father William wrote and directed films between 1914 and 1932, her uncle was Cecil B. de Mille—did not end up in the film business. It is a testament, in fact, to the power of live theatre at the time—she was born in 1905 and moved to Hollywood in 1914—when fame, fortune, and celebrity in the theatrical arts were still to be found on the stage, not the screen. Despite the glamour of the burgeoning film business, de Mille saw Anna Pavlova dance when she was thirteen years old, and resolved to duplicate that dramatic event.

Although neither her parents nor the culture considered dance a suitable pursuit for a young woman, she persevered, staging dramatic productions in her back yard and practicing on her own in her bathroom. Finally she was allowed to take dancing lessons because her sister did, due to the advice of a doctor on Margaret's fallen arches. To the absolute benefit of the worlds of both ballet and musical comedy, de Mille was terrible at ballet, her long torso, short arms and legs, and late start making it difficult for her to imitate the classic ballet style that dominated at the time. Unable to find work as a ballet dancer, she began the extraordinary process of choreographing for herself in recitals, concentrating on "character" pieces. Without a great deal of technical training, but with an extraordinary imagination, she danced wherever and whenever she could. Eventual training in London at Marie Rambert's Ballet Club did little for her dancing, but wonders for her creativity, as that Depression-era studio was a hotbed of young choreographers such as Frederick Ashton and Anthony Tudor. Finally she joined the original *American Ballet Theatre*, where she choreographed *Black Ritual* in 1940, the first ballet to use black dancers (whom she had to recruit from outside the company). Her next piece, *Three Virgins and a Devil*, is still performed today.

But it is with the piece she did for Ballet Russe de Monte Carlo—in America at the Met because of the war in Europe—that claims a place in musical comedy history. To American composer Aaron Copland's music, she choreographed *Rodeo*, a western ballet and, more to the point, an early story- and character-driven ballet. (It was a character, the pioneer girl, that she had been developing since her first concert years before. She premiered an early version, *The Rodeo*, in 1938 in London with dancers utterly unfamiliar with the American West, or American energy.) Still desperate to be a dancer at thirty-seven, and unaware of her future as a choreographer, she danced the lead. Legend has it the ballet received twenty-two curtain calls. Rodgers and Hammerstein and the Theatre Guild brass, then about to stage a musical version of the western folk play *Green Grow the Lilacs* to be called *Away We Go*, saw it and hired her to be the choreographer on their new musical. Which changed its name out of town to *Oklahoma!*

Perhaps de Mille felt some trepidation, since she had already been fired twice from Broadway assignments (*Flying Colors*, a Dietz and Schwartz revue, and *Hooray for What!* with a score by Arlen and Harburg). Her arrogance and ego, her obsessive melodramatics, her argumentiveness when a choreographer was low man on the totem pole always got in the way.

She spent hours in preparation. She insisted on good dancers with a variety of looks, upsetting her male collaborators, who were accustomed to casting beautiful chorus girls, including their own "personal favorites." She was autocratic and demanding, in constant conflict with the director. Ultimately only Rodgers stood up for her work. She choreographed what she claimed to be twice as many dances as ended up in the show. All were solidly staged and entertaining, but it was with the "Dream Ballet" that she became famous: Laurey's "psychological" dream that features the two men in her life—Curly and Jud, as well as dancing cowhands and saloon girls—and delineates Laurey's fear of going to the picnic with the wrong one.

If self-determination plays a large part in the life of any artist, de Mille's long years of study, of dancing and choreographing, are an extreme example. The exuberant, aggressive, diminutive

(5´1˝), fiery redhead who had come from a long line of artistic personalities on both sides of her family had pursued dance and choreography against all obstacles. With her intense passion and individual approach she would help ballet become American and infuse musical theatre with dance as never before. In the Broadway musical form, she had found a place for the character dances that had been her personal style. For fourteen years a prophet without honor, she had found, in one night, her calling, her genre, and her audience.

Much has been written about the sudden and outstanding success of *Oklahoma!* With movies still a novelty and television still in the future, Broadway was the center of popular culture. A war-weary America—it was 1943—embraced the pure American spirit embodied in the story. The homespun dialogue and romantic story, the turning of a western frontier territory into a state, was a last nostalgic look at a fast-disappearing aspect of America. Richard Rodgers, writing away from the witty, sophisticated lyrics of Hart for his first score with the romantic, sincere Hammerstein, rose to new heights of melody. For the first time, a theatre score reflected its setting, incorporating western rhythms and harmonies. The warm-hearted story avoided the girls, gags, and dancing Tiller lines inserted willy-nilly into previous musical comedies—it was labeled a "musical play" in publicity—and John Raitt was a newly discovered, and rare, hero with masculinity and a rich baritone. All true. But what comes down to us most of all is the lack of dances thrown in purely for entertainment's sake, and their replacement with the character-derived, plot-oriented work of de Mille. One previous musical (*On Your Toes*) had integrated its dances, but *Oklahoma!* did it with such conviction, confidence, smoothness, and success, that to "musical comedy"—never put entirely in the shade, and why should it be?—was added "musical theatre." With the addition of dance as a dramatic device, Wagner's desire for a "total" theatre was completely realized.

Hammerstein called for a first-act finale that was a dream ballet in his script, but de Mille's version was in fact a nightmare, going much further into the psyche of the characters than Hammerstein had ever imagined. (The sexual fascination Laurey has for Jud comes from the sexual repression of de Mille, who was raised in a home where her mother did not know a name for her sexual parts. And de Mille had been in Freudian analysis.)

In her very next show, de Mille's contribution was even greater. *One Touch of Venus*, however (music by Kurt Weill, lyrics by new-to-Broadway poet Ogden Nash, and starring Mary Martin), wasn't a show destined to go down in history. It ran a respectable 567 performances, and has never been revived. (*Oklahoma!* would eventually run 2,212, with three Broadway revivals and thousands of productions worldwide.) The lack of a singular vision by its director Elia Kazan, who had never experienced the *sturm und drang* of a musical before, and a lack of comedy in the dialogue and clarity in the book by S.J. Perelman, who had primarily written magazine humor, curtailed its popularity. De Mille's work, however, was more extensive, more plot-oriented, and richer than ever before. "Forty Minutes for Lunch" was just what the title suggests, with the statue-come-to-life character experiencing the street outside Rockefeller Center. "Venus in Ozone Heights," the show's finale, in which our heroine has to make up her mind whether to stay in our world or return to the bacchanalian world of Dionysus, ended the musical, and it was de Mille's alteration of the ending from sad to happy that improved the show. Her dances were even more integrated into the plot than in *Oklahoma!*

Her "Civil War Ballet" in *Bloomer Girl* was another battle with producers, who wanted it cut for its depressing, anti-war depiction of women waiting for soldiers who are not coming home. But its reception in Philadelphia assured its place at the end of that musical.

By the spring of 1945, de Mille had four hit musicals running on Broadway. Shortly she added *Brigadoon*, with a handful of her best dances yet. Curiously, in spite of her work, Lerner and Loewe (*Brigadoon's* authors) declined to work with her again. Their next show was *My Fair Lady*. In fact, the bulk of her success had covered only five years. She was unable to make the transition to director that the new musical era—which she helped invent—required. A prickly personality and a homophobe, she was unable to work in the friendly collaboration that would have made authors and producers want to work with her again. She was unable to work in the jazz idiom that was rapidly overtaking Broadway choreography. According to its composer Jule Styne, de Mille's dances for *Gentlemen Prefer Blondes* were "all wrong."

There were both dream and real ballets for the prickly, autocratic de Mille in many more musicals. She was hired often to do her thing. One landmark assignment was the Rodgers and Hammerstein musical *Allegro*. It became the first musical ever directed by its choreographer, and the director-choreographer was born. The show had problems and ran only ten months, and that due to the box office advance triggered by the enormous popularity of Rodgers and Hammerstein. With a cast of 100, an overwhelming set complete with turntables (do they *ever* work at the first performance?), a weak score (not driven by any more interesting milieu than small-town America), and second-act troubles (Hammerstein having gone into rehearsal not quite ready, because the Rodgers and Hammerstein organization had become so busy with producing chores), *Allegro* became a disappointment to all, with de Mille having to give up overseeing the entire production. (Hammerstein took over the scenes, and Rodgers pitched in with the musical numbers.)

De Mille might have become the first superdirector, even after the *Allegro* fiasco, but her ego and personality got in the way. Unable to place her dances at the service of the larger show, unable to direct—because the songs and scenes meant nothing to her—de Mille never put together a real work of art for the musical stage, only pieces. She had, however, pointed the way, and those who came after—Robbins and Kidd, Fosse and Bennett—walked through the door. She gave them dance as the final tool for the ultimate musical, and they created the era of the auteur.

She seldom again directed. But her staging continued in many musicals and in ballet, until a debilitating stroke in 1975 curtailed her work. Recovering, she lectured ("Conversations on the Dance") and wrote wonderful books (ten in all) until her death in 1993. Some of her ballets are still in the repertory of companies world-wide, and *Oklahoma!*, her only significant film work, is a good way to see the dancing that revolutionized the American musical. (Her relationship with Rodgers and Hammerstein had become so rancorous that they hired Rod Alexander to choreograph the film of *Carousel*.) Yet in the end, she had, single-handedly, created the prototype of American theatre dance.

Jerome Robbins

"Jerry's artistic ruthlessness was combined with real sadism."
—Stephen Sondheim

No one was more intimidating than Robbins, a man whom most of his comrades claimed was an unmitigated bastard in dealing with people, but with whom they would gladly work again for his pure genius. ("If I go to hell, I will not be afraid of the devil. Because I have worked with Jerome Robbins." —Mel Tomlinson, dancer with the New York City Ballet)

Finding his way into dance with a stubborn determination against both a late start and the image of male dancers, Robbins was a dancer known for his musical abilities. He had been a piano prodigy. (It would drive Bernstein crazy when Robbins would stand over him at the piano, listen to a new composition, and tell him to change a note or chord.) When de Mille was casting a ballet, Robbins was recommended to her as a dancer "who could count anything." The ambitious dancer eventually submitted a ballet scenario of his own to the directors at American Ballet Theatre. It was accepted, and when he choreographed *Fancy Free*, his reputation was established. The theatricality of that first significant work had been honed by his several summers at Camp Tamiment, the bungalow colony that in the 1930s hired many soon-to-be-famous young theatre people to put on their weekly entertainments. When that ballet was turned into the full-length Broadway musical *On the Town*, he became a much sought-after choreographer in both worlds.

His body of work in the theatre is unparalleled. David Merrick once said that his "three favorite musicals were *West Side Story*,

Fiddler on the Roof, and *Gypsy,* one of which I had the pleasure of producing." It had to be pointed out to him that Robbins had directed and choreographed all three.

Robbins, Bernstein, Laurents, and Sondheim were what is known in academic sociology as a "hot group," talented people who found and fed off each other, creating both what they have called an "exhilarating experience" and the synergy that causes collaborative art to rise above individual contributions. They were not unaware of this. While out of town with *West Side Story,* Bernstein wrote, "If all goes as well in New York as it has on the road, we will have proved something very big indeed and maybe changed the face of the American musical theatre." It did, and they did.

Robbins' contribution to the American musical falls into two categories. In writing both *On the Town* and their subsequent collaboration *West Side Story,* Robbins and Bernstein sketched out whole sections of the plot that would be told in dance. Nothing like this had ever been done, at least in so wholesale a way, though *On Your Toes* had featured two story sequences specifically meant to be staged by Balanchine. In contrast to the practice at the time, in which rehearsal pianists arranged dance music for the choreographer based on the composer's songs, Bernstein wrote original symphonic pieces. Thus was dance so thoroughly integrated into the actual text of the developing story, even before rehearsals began. The unique show was to be a "ballet/opera": impressionistic, with spare dialogue, the sets abstract and nonlinear. (In fact, it was designer Oliver Smith who refused the "in one" curtain that would mask scene changes, and forced the cinematic, fluid staging that became a Robbins—and modern musical—hallmark.)

And his vocabulary. Where de Mille had bent and stretched the vocabulary of classic ballet to imitate cowboys and dance hall girls, Robbins worked in the other direction, first studying the movement of the characters in their milieu—for *West Side* he observed the teenagers in the neighborhood, for *The King and I* he studied Cambodian dance with an expert, for *Fiddler* he attended Jewish weddings—then created a vocabulary from his impressions. This resulted in an even greater character-driven dance vocabulary. In *West Side Story* the opening sequence, "Prologue," is a choreographed battle over the turf between the two gangs. "The Dance at the Gym" is precisely that, each of the clashing cultures working in their own style, challenging each other for predominance on the floor. "Cool" is built on the tensions within the teenagers; their inner turmoil and explosive rage. *Fiddler on the Roof*'s "To Life" takes place in the local inn, in a small village in Russia in 1905, as the men celebrate an engagement. The subtle combination of drinking and dancing, the entrance of the Russians in their own style (reminiscent of steps we know from their folk ballets), and the drunken tableau as a climax, adds up to more than a dance, but a full scene. The marriage sequence combines the famous and authentic "bottle dance" and a whipping around of the back into the snapping of the fingers overhead that authentically duplicates the frenzy of Jewish folk dances. Included is a unique plot point: a radical young man has the audacity to cross the rope that separates the sexes and ask a young girl to dance, and, once more, "tradition" is under attack. For *Gypsy*, Robbins recreated vaudeville, burlesque, and stripping as Louise makes her way from one to the other. Even when returning to pure dance—after *Fiddler*

Robbins became a full-time choreographer and associate director with New York City Ballet—his ballets were often infused with character, plot, comedy, and ambience.

Robbins added directing to his skills with *Look Ma, I'm Dancing* in 1948 and unlike Cole and de Mille was able to put his own dances at the service of the overall musical. He was deeply interested in directing, was a member of the Actor's Studio Director's Lab, and directed a handful of plays as well as musicals.

Another contribution Robbins made was the richness of his ensembles. Prior to his shows, chorus dancers could come on as generic members of the local community. We're in an office? Bring on the secretaries and executives. We're on a beach? Bring on the bathing beauties. Nothing wrong with that, precisely. But Robbins, with *West Side* and then *Fiddler*, insisted that everyone in the cast have a character. He asked each singer and dancer in the chorus to write up their character's biography. Everyone in *West Side* had a name and a profile, a place in the hierarchy of the gang. Each villager in *Fiddler* had his place, his occupation, in the village.

It is with Robbins' success that the director-choreographer fully arrived, and it is with Robbins' shows, including the classics *West Side Story*, *Gypsy*, and *Fiddler on the Roof*, that we see for the first time the true, complete, detailed integration of the American book musical.

After *Fiddler*, he didn't return to Broadway until 1989, when he staged a medley of his musical numbers from decades of shows, titled *Jerome Robbins' Broadway*. Indeed it was, from *On the Town* in 1944 to *Fiddler on the Roof* in 1964. (As a testament to the success of his various musicals, there have been nineteen fully staged Broadway revivals of musicals he directed or choreographed since then.) This *Broadway* was a sensation, though his showman's instinct and unerring ability to entertain caused him to create a series of medleys around each show, little mini-dramas that, for young people who were unfamiliar with the original, may have been a bit confusing. The lavishness with which the original sets and costumes were recreated, and the size of the cast, and the extraordinary twenty-two-week rehearsal period (most musicals rehearse six) created a high breakeven that kept the show from running as long as it deserved, and kept it from touring widely; a great loss. Nevertheless, the variety of great theatre songs and the unique style of theatre choreography Robbins had invented made it a remarkable journal of a golden age.

The most famous anecdote about Jerome Robbins has been told by many dancers in many of his shows, all of whom profess to having been there. He was energetically giving notes onstage, and backing up, unaware of how close he was coming to the edge of the stage. No one said a word, and he fell into the orchestra pit. This legendary story is usually told with the understanding that Robbins' rehearsal behavior was so vicious that no one cared to warn him. There is another point of view, however: that given his hold over any company, when Mr. Robbins was speaking, no one dared breathe.

Robbins' choreography for *West Side Story*, the exquisite story ballet "the Small House of Uncle Thomas" from *The King and I*, and a television version of *Peter Pan* can be seen on film. More of his work can be seen in various television specials and, with appropriate permissions, on video tape in the dance collection of the New York Public Library at Lincoln Center.

Michael Kidd

Old gypsy joke: though versions abound, I'll go with the one I first heard. Onna White was rehearsing a dance number, became frustrated, and finally shouted at the boys, "Will you please dance like you have some balls!" Whereupon one of them turned to the stage manager and lisped, "Props!"

While none of the choreographers on this list ever promoted effeminate male dancers, they seldom promoted masculinity either. Robbins' gangs in *West Side Story*, particularly the virile Puerto Ricans, were strong. His engagement dance, "To Life", and "Bottle Dance" and "Wedding Dance" in *Fiddler on the Roof* were rich in the male characters of the village. Yet even those wonderful dance shows for men don't celebrate the male dancer so much as express the story line. Champion's work was androgynous. He worked in Busby Berkeley styles, great swooping troops of bodies flying in and out, or lined up in patterns that echoed the Rockettes, his vocabulary mostly that of vaudeville. Fosse concentrated on his girls, the boys in *Pippin* neutered and unnecessary. An exception was Swen Swenson's startling strip tease in *Little Me*, "I've Got Your Number." Jack Cole, who had pioneered sex in dance, particularly in his concert and nightclub work, gave all his dancers a fierce sexuality equally. Then came Michael Kidd.

Hard on the heels of his ballet career—one of his best roles was one of the sailors in Robbins' *Fancy Free*—he began choreographing Broadway musicals. Shortly thereafter he executed those chores on *Guys and Dolls*, and came up with the "Crapshooter's Ballet." The "Guys" of Damon Runyon's Broadway were gymnastic, masculine, and athletic, never overly precise but always strong and sharp. His work is preserved in the film version, but his choreography for the original film musical *Seven Brides for Seven Brothers* tops them all—it's considered the best dancing in film musical history. In one of the numbers, Kidd pits prissy townsmen against the raw masculinity of the farm boys. No contest. Another, "Lonesome Polecat," physicalizes the loneliness of the brothers in a working-in-the-snow song and ballet. You couldn't dramatize "horny" in those days, but if you could have, it would be there. Kidd even managed, in the "Girl Hunt Ballet" for the film *The Bandwagon,* to give Fred Astaire, as a noir detective, balls. Not easy. Astaire's charm was always more Edwardian-man-about-town than masculine.

Choreographers depend on writers. They can only stage the dramatic ideas that already exist in the script, though in the hurly-burly world of assembling a musical, there is often room for invention. Their work always risks being cut. (Remember that the director wanted to excise de Mille's "Dream Ballet" from *Oklahoma!* because it gave away coming plot points.) Not too many musicals have featured leading men who dance. The great exception, *Pal Joey,* featured Gene Kelly, and then ABT alumni Harold Lang in the revival, but sexuality hadn't yet reared its randy head in Broadway rhythm. Against those odds, Kidd forged dances, and shows, in which men were men, leaping high, stout-hearted, and passionate about their dolls.

Not to say that Kidd didn't do as well with women. *Li'l Abner*'s girls are probably the sexiest characters in any musical. There, in the "Sadie Hawkins Day Ballet," in which the girls get to marry any man they can catch, Kidd created comic interplay between the ladies of the ensemble and the men that just isn't found in any other musical. Although the films of *Guys and Dolls* and *Li'l Abner* are often considered by film critics as "overly stylized," that's greatly to the advantage of theatre fans, as one can see there the unique style Kidd brought to the dancing of both men and women. It's simply stupefyin'.

Gower Champion

"I never thought that Gower was a great choreographer, but he was a great concept person. Whatever story value needed to be illuminated, be it text or song, he was able to do it. In his four or five really great hit shows, the scenery danced, the lighting danced." —Marge Champion

If the other choreographers on our list had all been successful dancers first, Champion was something else. He had been a national celebrity.

With his first partner Jeanne Tyler, the sixteen-year-old Gower won a dance contest. The award was a week's engagement at the classy Coconut Grove supper club in Los Angeles, where they were so popular they signed with MCA, and soon became successful on the nightclub circuit. Prohibition had ended, and throughout the 1930s supper clubs were next only to Broadway as America's cultural playground. Champion was tall, handsome, and suave, a true heir to Fred Astaire, starring live in the most exclusive supper clubs from New York to Chicago to Hollywood. While few dance teams featured the male, Champion, as had Astaire, dominated with his charisma.

Following a stint in the Coast Guard, where he appeared in the musical revue *Tars and Spars* and staged shows aboard a troop transport, and because Tyler in the meantime had married and retired, he went out on his own as an actor and dancer.

That year was unsuccessful. Not an experienced actor, and without the strict training that would have made him attractive to other choreographers, he found little work. Then he teamed up with his dance teacher's daughter, Marge Belcher. Aware that other choreographers couldn't provide them with the quality numbers they wanted, Gower began to direct the act, choosing the music, choreographing clever dances, organizing the costumes and lights. Marge and Gower Champion (they married) shortly became famous, not only starring in posh clubs, but adding television, which was just coming in, and MGM films to their credits throughout the 1950s. As a dance act, they had been back and forth to Broadway as well, first brought there by Robert Alton.

In the flush of youth and success, Gower successfully managed his career as a performer. By the time he reached his thirties he was pursuing every opportunity to direct, which he did in numerous television shows.

Gower's "story dances" for their act kept him right in line with the developing style of Broadway musical choreography, and when he began to choreograph musicals—*Lend An Ear* (1948), *Make a Wish* (1951)—his dances were often driven by story and character.

By age forty it was inevitable. A tour of Russia sponsored by Ed Sullivan was the last appearance of the Marge and Gower dance act. But Gower was prepared. He had already signed to direct and choreograph a Broadway musical called *Let's Go Steady*, devoted to the new rock and roll craze. A series of name changes—*Love and*

Kisses; *The Day They Took Birdie Away*; *Going Steady*; *Goodbye Birdie, Goodbye*—would lead to *Bye Bye Birdie*.

The rest—*Carnival*, *Hello, Dolly!*, *I Do! I Do!*, and then a rash of less distinguished scripts, and then *42nd Street*—is history. His career was the last of an era when a producer (David Merrick) and director, each alone, each with total creative control over their particular domain, could mount a large Broadway musical. (Here are the producing credits for the 2005 Tony Award winner for Best Musical: produced by Boyett Ostar Productions, The Shubert Organization (Gerald Schoenfeld: Chairman; Philip J. Smith: President; Robert E. Wankel: Executive Vice President), Arielle Tepper, Stephanie McClelland, Lawrence Horowitz, Élan V. McAllister, Allan S. Gordon, Independent Presenters Network, Roy Furman, GRS Associates, Jam Theatricals, TGA Entertainment, Ltd., Clear Channel Entertainment.)

Even within the less corporate world Champion functioned in, his greatest talent was the exercise of power. And an eye for musical numbers that built. And built and built. Although he failed as often as he succeeded (*A Broadway Musical*, *Rockabye Hamlet*, *Prettybelle*) and had several also-rans (*The Happy Time*, *Sugar*, *Irene*, *Mack & Mabel*), his work was always crisp, clear, and wildly entertaining. He usually marshaled large choruses in numbers that came off like the inner workings of a Swiss watch. And just when you thought you'd seen the biggest number in the show, he unfolded a bigger one.

To the extent that he was almost the last of the choreographers who could afford large casts—or, possibly, knew what to do with them—he was the last great old-fashioned stager, descended from the "dance directors" of elaborate revue days. But choreographers then dealt only with the standard vocabulary. (So standard, in fact, that a producer could hire eight, sixteen, or thirty-two girls as a package from the English studio run by John Tiller, and insert a prepackaged number into his show.) It was Champion's talent to turn this kind of dance to the service of the story.

Between *Hello, Dolly!* and *42nd Street* Gower attempted to stage a number of musicals for which he simply did not have the dramatic theatre background, in each case wowing the critics with one or more showstopping numbers but failing to conceive the show with a singular vision appropriate to the story. Huge photographic projections and large chorus numbers overwhelmed the original small, sentimental story of *The Happy Time.* Sweeping musical numbers all had to be cut from *Sugar,* as the Billy Wilder farce, almost in spite of Champion, gradually came forward. The drama of romance, drugs, death, and regrets, which some fans consider Michael Stewart's best book and Jerry Herman's best score, was overwhelmed when he mounted too many Mack Sennett numbers in *Mack & Mabel,* ultimately unable to compete with the screen versions. Two unique musicals, *Prettybelle* ("A Lively Tale of Rape and Resurrection") and *Rockabye Hamlet* (the kind of musical that makes young audiences bravo and critics shudder), flopped, with Champion unable to find a style, other than his usual, that could deliver the dark material with consistency. Finally, with *42nd Street,* he had the perfect Champion show: a cardboard story that cardboard characters flew through to get to the next big dance number.

A showman more than a choreographer, his vocabulary often came from Marge and his assistants. A remarkable string of numbers opened many of Champion's musicals—see Chapter Six—but his most remarkable talent was an ability to create further numbers in his shows that topped the opening.

None of his successful shows were arrived at easily. Weeks of rehearsal and endless out-of-town tryouts and delayed previews characterized all his shows, during which he made change after change, sometimes putting in new numbers that were thrown out after one viewing. (All his shows went considerably over budget, but Merrick, his frequent producer, always cannily built the excess into the original budget without telling him.)

Abandoned by his father as a toddler and raised entirely by a bitter, cold, domineering mother (whose Christian Scientist beliefs almost killed him at least once when she refused him medical treatment), he grew up masking his emotions with an aloof bearing. Walking into even a rehearsal impeccably attired, the dazzling smile, the tall stature impressed everyone. Perhaps few directors could ever have worked so many times (seven) with the irascible, disruptive, Machiavellian Merrick. Champion, however, managed to keep Merrick at bay most of the time with his secretive rehearsals (not even the authors were allowed in the rehearsal room) and constant changes. All the authors and composers he worked with wrote more scenes and songs for their show with Champion then for any others in their careers.

Lack of an education both academically—he had dropped out of high school—and in the full range of dance—he had very little training compared to other choreographers—limited his approach to shows. His shows flowed, but when confronted with "book problems" he was utterly at sea, making change after change in shows that were not going well, yet often not focusing on a singular vision or concept and overlooking a story's true dramatic values while spending all his energy and most of the rehearsal time on the dances.

Although he never pursued serious drama and was in fact hopelessly at sea with actors, he did pursue the "continuous action" of Oscar Hammerstein with a passion that led to some of the most amazing stagecraft in musical theatre.

His career was in decline when he staged the throwback musical *42nd Street*. Based on the 1933 film choreographed by Busby Berkeley, the 1980 stage version—a match made in heaven for Champion's style of staging—was the most "old-fashioned" of all his shows. It was a smash hit, running eight and a half years originally and nearly four more in revival. He went out on top—pure musical comedy as silly and formulaic as any he had ever done, but with spectacular staging, the size and efficiency of which we may never see again.

In a telling example of the passion that the theatre offers, Champion knew he was dying (of a rare blood disease) when he was offered *42nd Street*. The doctors told him he could probably live three more years, but not if he placed himself under the stress of another Broadway musical. He chose to do the musical. He died opening night.

Bob Fosse

During the golden age of Broadway musical comedy, hundreds of dancers would turn out for an audition for a new Broadway musical, especially when it was to be choreographed by one of the legendary greats in the field. When Jerome Robbins held an audition, his opening remarks to the gathered dancers went something like this:

"This is a difficult show. You have to be technically proficient. If you're not, don't waste my time, and don't embarrass yourself. Leave now." The temperature dipped several degrees. When Bob Fosse held an audition, his first speech was along these lines: "I want to thank you for coming. I know auditioning is a difficult process; I wish I could hire all of you. If I eliminate you today, don't hesitate to come back next time, and try again." Fosse's warm love for dancers (which didn't extend to producers or writers) evidenced itself in all his shows, which were always rooted in dance.

Nearly the polar opposite of Robbins, Bob Fosse was beloved by his dancers, but difficult on his producers and writers. Albert Hague said that working with Fosse was like going to the best dentist in town: it hurt like hell while you were there, but afterwards, you're glad you went.

Fosse began his dancing with tap, and though it didn't feature in too many of his shows (there was an exquisite section in his "Sing, Sing, Sing" number in *Dancin'*, and a soft shoe valentine to Fred Astaire in that show's "I Want to Be a Dancin' Man"), tap's rhythms formed Fosse's immense musicality, and led to the neat syncopations he often utilized. (Theatre legend: when staging "A Secretary Is Not a Toy" for *How to Succeed*, he was frustrated by the lilting waltz rhythm of the original Frank Loesser song. Without telling Loesser, he and the dance arranger altered the rhythm to a much quicker 12/8, changing the whole feeling of the song. Terrified, they finally invited Loesser to take a look. He approved.)

By the age of fifteen Fosse was leading a dual identity. A good and popular student in high school, he would grab his hidden dance clothes after school and slip away to class and, eventually, jobs on the local Rotary circuit. With a partner (they called themselves the Riff Brothers) he found engagements in burlesque houses. Though Fosse has memorialized his own coming-of-age in a burlesque house with a scene in his autobiographical film *All That Jazz*, he doesn't mention that he was, at that age, named in an adultery suit by the husband of a woman in her thirties.

Anxious to become the next Gene Kelly, Fosse did get a Hollywood contract and appeared in a number of films, but the best of them featured dances he choreographed himself. (See the "Challenge Dance" he did with Tommy Rall in *My Sister Eileen*, the brief jazz routine within "From This Moment On" that he performed with Carol Haney in *Kiss Me Kate*, and "Who's Got the Pain" in *Damn Yankees* for wonderful records of his work as both choreographer and dancer.)

Early in his Broadway career, Fosse teamed with the inestimable Gwen Verdon. She was the lascivious red-headed dancer who exploded out of the Jack Cole chorus to solo fame in *Can-Can*, and with whom Fosse spent the rest of his life in fruitful collaboration. (During that ideal artistic partnership they also married and separated.) Even when Verdon wasn't in his shows, her ghost hovered over them; Leland Palmer filled in with a Verdonesque character in *Pippin* and portrayed another Verdon stand-in in Fosse's autobiographical film *All That Jazz*. Eventually he transferred his affection to the entire chorus, and his girls roamed his stages with a Lola-like eroticism in many musical numbers. From the presentational hookers in "Hey, Big Spender" from *Sweet Charity* to the pastoral sex ballet "With You" in *Pippin* to the orgy in *All That Jazz*, he pursued that rara avis in musical comedy—erotic choreography.

Biographically speaking, the most accurate thing to say about Fosse is that he put his oversexed personal life into his work, creating the most erotic dances of the golden age (leading to a virtual orgy in *All That Jazz* called "Take Off With Us"). He can also be accused of sleeping his way to the top, as he left one wife for another with greater access to the highest echelons of show businesss (for the record: chorus girl Mary Ann Niles to supporting actress Joan McCracken to star Gwen Verdon). Having arrived at the pinnacle of success, he worked his way back down to chorus girls, but glibly refused to be monogamous. (His biographical film wants us to feel sorry for a guy who drinks too much, smokes too much, does too many drugs, beds too many women, and is wildly successful in his career.)

His dances were collected in *Fosse: A Celebration*, which opened on Broadway in 1999. *Fosse* was a wildly entertaining evening, and a revelation. Great American musical theatre dance hadn't been exhibited on the stage since 1975 (*A Chorus Line*), with the exception of *Jerome Robbins' Broadway*. Fosse, who of all the musical theatre choreographers of the golden age was the most individual, with his vaudeville style, burlesque pelvis, asymmetrical limbs, and erotic slithers, was posthumously represented by a large company of extremely skilled, hard-working dancers who performed a thirty-year panorama of his creations from his first showstopper, "Steam Heat" from *Pajama Game,* to his great swing concerto, "Sing, Sing, Sing" from *Dancin'.* Newcomers to his work were blown away with the razzle-dazzle of it all.

Those familiar with most of Fosse's work in its original form, after impatiently waiting eleven years since his death to see again some of the best dances Broadway ever produced, had to be somewhat disappointed.

For some unaccountable reason, all of his dances were recast in the mood of the last, darkest, most pessimistic period of Fosse's life. This exhibition of his career is tantamount to exhibiting paintings from Mark Rothko's late black period only, and then expecting an audience new to his work to understand his full life's achievement. All-black costumes on an all-black set managed to make Fosse's entire career seem even narrower than it really was, a nimble achievement considering that he was the narrowest of stylists to begin with, a virtually self-taught tapper, hat on head, props for distraction, and heated libido defining his slim vocabulary.

But in Fosse's thirty-year career he used those tools for maximum impact in twelve shows and nine films, in the end claiming, from the Broadway musicals *Pajama Game* and *Damn Yankees* to the films *Lenny* and *Star 80*, the widest artistic arc of any choreographer of the twentieth century.

Fosse's drive was in dance. Many of his shows featured dances that far outshone the rest of the musical, and didn't feature the degree of integration that Robbins had developed. He nevertheless inherited that form, and both in *Sweet Charity* and *Pippin* (in which the staging was the star), the scenes, songs, and dances flow along beautifully. Neither "Steam Heat" (*Pajama Game*) nor "Who's Got the Pain?" (*Damn Yankees*) are remotely integrated, being simply entertainments within the story ("While we're waiting, here's a number . . . "). Yet both stop their shows, proving that good old-fashioned song and dance could still—I'd say *can* still if there were a choreographer alive who could do it—bring an audience to its feet.

Not unlike many artists, Fosse harbored inseparable, unquench-able desires—to be loved, to achieve, to succeed—which drove him to riskier and riskier creativity, and which he attempted to satiate with women, booze, and drugs. The only person ever to win the famous triple crown for directing—he won the Oscar (*Cabaret*), Tony (*Pippin*), and Emmy (*Liza With a Z*) all in the same year—he checked into the Payne-Whitney clinic for "depression" three weeks later! After his film *Star 80* tanked, he never really recovered his early Broadway esprit. No one could tell him that the brilliant film of an ugly, dark story wasn't going to be a crowd pleaser, and the dichotomy gradually tore him apart; one little voice prompting him to give 'em the old razzle-dazzle, the other pushing him to turn his own insides out in pursuit of art. It isn't often that the two coincide, and once in a lifetime (his film of *Cabaret*) is probably once more than most artists experience.

The contradiction between show business, which was his art, and art, which was his business, drove him crazy. He whined that the *New York Times* never said a kind word about him, even while *Pippin* and *Dancin'* ran just under five years apiece, but he didn't cut off his ear. Instead, he dressed all in black, refused to give up his hedonistic lifestyle even after a triple coronary bypass, and curled his stick-thin body into an ever-greater question mark. He withdrew from the collaboration of equals, mounting his last show by himself, using pre-existing songs and his own libretto. Yet there were colorful numbers in even that show, *Big Deal*, that exploded with his enthusiasm for the dancer in the dance.

Fosse: A Celebration, however, is too dark to be called a celebra-tion, and too slim to be a fair appreciation. Since the numbers are not in chronological order, and there is no biographical material about Fosse, the show is without even the semblance of a rising line of dramatic action, something good revues must invent. Without a concept, or even a continuum of ideas, the creators of the show have tried to find some subjective line by assembling the dances by type, and by linking them with "transitional choreography" in the Fosse style by one of his protegés. The transitional choreography only serves to deprive the numbers of a strong beginning and end, a structure he was great with and one that defines the musical comedy dance number as distinctly as a good short story. A medley of trios, Fosse's favorite grouping, serves only to make them all blend together, as if he had endlessly repeated himself from the bebop of "Steam Heat" to the devilish "Manson Trio." In fact he did more for the trio idea than the Andrews Sisters.

If the final era of Fosse's creativity comprised his fascination with the angel of death and his tortured ruminations on life as an unhappy and frustrating alternative to show business ("To be on the wire is life. Everything else is just waiting."—tightropist Karl Wallenda, who Fosse quoted in *All That Jazz*), he arrived there via a brighter perspective. The wild exuberance of their "Once a Year Day" picnic from *Pajama Game*, when the factory workers criss-cross the stage with humor and athleticism, the trio of dance hall girls leaping on rooftops demanding that "There's Gotta Be Something Better Than This" in *Sweet Charity*, and Swen Swenson's striptease in *Little Me*, "I've Got Your Number," (the first two available on DVD, thank goodness) are all great examples. (And all missing from *Fosse: A Celebration*. Missing also is *How to Succeed in Business Without Really Trying*, from which not a single number was extracted, even though it marked the apex of the young choreographer finding his own unique style of musical staging.)

The films *Cabaret* and *All That Jazz* are his musical legacy, and a production of *Pippin* was filmed live, though Fosse repudiated it. *Fosse: A Celebration* is available on DVD, and in it you can easily see the unique, showbiz style he forged in his dances. Without the full range of his work, however, *Fosse: A Celebration* only illustrates the depressingly sad angst of a man who had lived himself into a small dark corner, probably dying unaware that he had bequeathed the world a big bright epoch of entertainment.

Michael Bennett

Short choreographers often fall into quick, frenetic little patterns of steps they're good at. The result is a lot of awkward, frantic choreography for the average, taller dancer. The exception was Michael Bennett, whose eye was for whom was dancing and not for himself in the mirror. A step on every beat eliminates variety and syncopation. Less is more. Just as Sondheim likes to compose away from the piano to avoid his fingers falling into overused favorite patterns, choreographers need to do much of their preparation away from the rehearsal room.

White-hot ambition and tons of childhood experience propelled Bennett into choreography. Mature well beyond his years, he earned his first Tony nomination at the age of twenty-three. He ended up a choreographer with a stellar ability to direct and a keen eye for showmanship, even within his desire for the Robbins-influenced integration he worshipped.

The diminutive Italian dancer dropped out of high school to dance in the European production of *West Side Story* under the direction of Jerome Robbins, and the unbroken line continued.

Bennett danced in only three Broadway musicals for other choreographers before he choreographed *A Joyful Noise* and *Henry,
Sweet Henry*, both of which closed early; yet for both he received
Tony nominations for Best Choreography (in an age when there
was significant competition each season). Then came *Promises,
Promises*, for which he not only staged the showstopping Act One
closing dance but, more significantly, staged less-obvious numbers
such as "She Likes Basketball," "Where Can You Take a Girl?,"
and "Grapes of Roth" with the remarkable combination of subtle
integration and entertaining pizzazz—satisfying both techniques at
once—that would mark his career. He increased this with musical
staging for *Company* and *Follies* and *Coco*; directed several plays,
notably the charming *Twigs*, guiding Sada Thompson in multiple
roles; saved *Seesaw* from ignominious failure in Detroit; and then
went into workshop for his penultimate achievement.

Integration. One would have thought that by 1974, that concept
would have been complete. *West Side Story* had opened seventeen
years earlier. Surely no one could have envisioned the totality of
integration, the synergistic result, of *A Chorus Line*. Perhaps not
even Bennett, who worked through a long "workshop" process
until he arrived at a finished product.

It was no coincidence that *A Chorus Line* was built around an
audition. Bennett's auditions had for years included singing and
acting for his dancers. A child of the a musical theatre that had
already seen years of musical numbers well integrated into the
text of their shows, Bennett knew no other form. It was normal
procedure among the writers he worked with. Bennett's talent was
to stop a show with a dazzling dance number without violating
that form.

Working on *Promises, Promises*, Bennett had assiduously avoided a bring-on-the-girls number—even to the point of turning "She Likes Basketball" into a solo for Jerry Orbach when the costume designer had already provided the possibility of basketball and cheerleader outfits for the chorus boys and girls. Yet out of town it became clear that the first act curtain was weak. It also became clear that the small part of a secretary was being cut, and Bennett's favorite dancer, Donna McKechnie, would soon be out of work. At that point Bennett staged "Turkey Lurkey Time," the showstopping dance-on-desktops that brought the first act curtain down to satisfying applause. Even then, he worked it up out of an office party, successfully integrating it into the story and the milieu.

While out of town with *Company*, Bennett's collaborators were bent on cutting Donna McKechnie's dance number, "Tick Tock," on the grounds that it was an isolated piece of dance that furthered no particular idea or story line. Given one last chance, Bennett created a new dance to a new arrangement by David Shire. They integrated dialogue from the previous scene, in which bachelor Bobby and his stewardess girlfriend were in bed. The subsequent solo dance—so successful with audiences that it couldn't be cut— illuminated the act of sex, at least from a woman's point of view, and provided a crowd-pleasing erotic moment in an otherwise almost neutered sequence of relationships.

It was in *Company*'s "Side by Side by Side" number, however, that Bennett demonstrated to anyone paying attention that his choreography alone could tell a story. By now more than one chronicler of the cause has remarked upon the extraordinary tap step that contains the whole theme of the musical. Five couples and bachelor Bob perform the number about the usefulness of pairing up. In a dance sequence, each of the couples executes a very brief call-and-response tap step, the simplest of vaudeville routines. (It had to be, as none of the principals were dancers.) This goes down the line until it reaches Bobby, who makes the statement, but receives no answer, not having a partner. A hollow echo resounds as the others dance on, and Bobby hesitates for a split second, reacting. Although the whole sequence goes by in a flash as the number continues to build to a climax, it was extremely effective in illuminating Bobby's dilemma through dance. A decade and a half later, George Furth told me that he had been wildly impressed by exactly the same moment the first time he saw it too, which was in rehearsal, because Furth was the author of *Company*.

Bennett was brilliant at character-driven work, and equally brilliant at structuring musical sequences to escalate to the point of goose-pimple revelations. More than once numbers of his—probably the most notable was "Who's That Woman?" in *Follies*—were celebrated as self-contained masterpieces. Bennett took two ideas—the showstopping entertainment and the integrated musical number— and combined them.

Though a retrospective of his work has yet to be mounted (and may never be, due to both financial and artistic obstacles), so many of his numbers—"Turkey Lurkey Time" from *Promises, Promises*; the fashion sequences from *Coco*; "Company," "Side by Side by Side," and "Tick Tock" from *Company*; "Who's That Woman?" and much of the Loveland sequence from *Follies*; "Seesaw" and "Ride Out the Storm" from *Seesaw*; "I Hope I Get It," "The Music and the Mirror," and "One" from *A Chorus Line*; several of the dance sequences from *Ballroom*; "Steppin' to the Bad Side" from

Dreamgirls—were showstoppers that would bring back the great days of the American musical as surely as did Robbins' revue.

Both Robbins and Bennett worked with an autocratic precision that defines the American rehearsal, and took the golden age of the American book musical to its highest level.

A Personal Story

I first saw *A Chorus Line* downtown, before it was reviewed, when it was just becoming famous by word-of-mouth among theatre people. The audience, utterly unprepared for the originality of the project, sat stunned for several moments before rising to its collective feet and bravoing its collective head off. I saw it several more times uptown at the Shubert with the original cast. Each time I gained an additional appreciation for the intricacies of the show in both writing and staging.

Then I was cast in one of Bennett's touring companies. I played the show for several weeks before I lost the feeling that I was running as fast as I could in front of a speeding train. Eventually, and with Michael's direct help, I believe I discharged my duties adequately. I settled in, and only then did the show's almost devious complexity become apparent to me.

When a dancer joined *A Chorus Line* he or she was given a script. On the first page was a blueprint of the stage, cross-hatched by recognizable lines. "Seams" in the floor were consistent, even on tour, because the show traveled with its own paneled stage floor. Up- and downstage "light pipes" were easy to spot if you glanced into the wings, and the white line painted downstage that the dancers stood on for their interviews was numbered: zero in the center, and one through eight radiating out. By reading the longitude and latitude details ("#6 left/2nd light pipe" or "#3 right/ middle seam"), a new dancer could tell precisely where his or her character should be at multiple, crucial points in the two-hour-and-twenty-minute musical. It was no substitute for rehearsal, but it evidenced both an extraordinary organization, and, more to the point here, a specificity in the staging more precise than earlier shows had ever dreamed of.

In trying to narrow the focus of this chapter to the choreographers that were instrumental in advancing the use of dance in musicals, I've omitted several choreographers who deserve notice for their contributions. Before he was the director of New York City Ballet, George Balanchine staged ballets for *On Your Toes*, *Babes in Arms*, and *I Married an Angel*. Albertina Rasch created three dream ballets for *Lady in the Dark*, a story ideally suited for them, as it was Moss Hart's take on psychoanalysis and the sequences were the dreams of a conflicted leading lady. All those shows preceded *Oklahoma!*

Hanya Holm staged *Kiss Me Kate* and *My Fair Lady*, and Onna White staged *The Music Man*, *Mame*, and *1776*. Peter Gennaro staged *Fiorello!*, *The Unsinkable Molly Brown*, and *Annie*. Though none of these musicals featured particularly distinguished dances, most—notably *The Music Man* and *1776*—featured musical numbers so cleverly staged they were well integrated.

Joe Layton choreographed or directed and choreographed *Barnum*, *Two by Two*, *George M!*, *No Strings* (where he introduced onstage musicians and actors moving the scenery), *Greenwillow*, *Sail Away*, and *The Sound of Music*. If his shows never featured galvanizing dances, they were well-integrated, fluid, and entertaining, with many original touches in the staging.

Herbert Ross choreographed *The Apple Tree*, *On a Clear Day You Can See Forever*, *Do I Hear a Waltz?*, *Anyone Can Whistle*, *I Can Get It for You Wholesale*, *The Gay Life*, *The Body Beautiful*, *House of Flowers*, *Three Wishes for Jamie*, and *A Tree Grows in Brooklyn* before his hugely successful career as a film director, which he launched by directing the musical sequences for the film version of *Funny Girl*, featuring textbook examples on how to film a song.

Many of these shows were exquisitely done, with just the right amount of dance, which was sometimes very little. They just weren't the kind of showcase the top choreographers wanted. Or their dances were cut when it was found, usually out of town, that they slowed down the show. However, the concept of integration does not require an equal use of all the contributing techniques; it only requires the *proper use* of each, as needed.

All the choreographers of the golden age developed their vocabulary along two lines: the character ballet and jazz of Agnes de Mille, Jack Cole, and Jerome Robbins, and the show dancers Robert Alton, Gower Champion, and Michael Bennett. All of them strove for integration, adapting their vocabulary to the characters and their content to the story.

Together they gradually invented what turned out to be a technique far more important than dance: musical staging. As early as the nineteenth century musicals were elaborately staged.

Photographs of early twentieth century operettas stagger the imagination. How did a chorus of over 100 "ladies and gentlemen of the ensemble" move about the stage effectively? Even the "tiny" Princess Theatre musicals featured an ensemble of two dozen. As the cost of shows increased and ensembles had to be trimmed (the beautifully staged *Pippin* featured a chorus of five boys and five girls), how the cast moved around and filled the stage became increasingly important. In concert with the increasing integration of the text, casts had to delight their audiences without elaborate sets or rows of chorus girls and boys in rich costumes. This trend reached its peak with *A Chorus Line*, when seventeen dancers in *rehearsal clothes* on a *bare stage* moved through an extraordinarily entertaining sequence of physical patterns.

Too often people think of the American book musical as something simple—at its best, some great songs sung by great singers in a show with exuberant dances and a happy ending. The commercial acceptance of *West Side Story*, *Man of La Mancha*, and *A Chorus Line* belie this. Not that the original formula, if professionally carried out, isn't wonderfully entertaining. But the issue isn't drama or comedy, happy or sad ending, or even, I hope, contemporary or classic American popular music. The issue is the slickness of the staging, the core, the final achievement of integration. The better the staging, the greater the musical. Many musical flops have fans of their scores, scores that sound as if the show ought to have been terrific. But the staging was mundane; the beautiful, often overproduced, sets cumbersome rather than helpful; the actors earthbound; the dancers either offstage or just extending a rhythm song with some gymnastics.

Great staging is important because you can't absorb all of a show's ideas in one sitting. Lyrics often fly by; musicals have great momentum.

Great staging—original, authentic, emotionally charged staging—is important because the theatre is a visual medium. You sit there, and you watch something new unfold before your eyes. No one who has witnessed the first assembling of the "line" in *A Chorus Line* can possibly not have gotten goose bumps. Likewise the slow build of the "Cool" number in Robbins' *West Side Story* choreography.

Here is the opening paragraph from Kenneth Tynan's review of the original production of *Gypsy*. (The English, having little forewarning in their own musicals, were quite stunned by the rise of the director-choreographer and the musicals imported from Broadway in those years.)

> Quite apart from considerations of subject matter, perfection of style can be profoundly moving in its own right. If anyone doubts that, he had better rush and buy a ticket for *Gypsy*, the first half of which brings together in effortless coalition all the arts of the American musical stage at their highest point of development. So smooth is the blending of skills, so precise the interlocking of song, speech, and dance, that the sheer contemplation of technique becomes a thrilling emotional experience.

Never mind that Tynan seems to have felt that the second act ("mere brilliance") was something of a letdown from the perfection of the first, primarily because Ethel Merman had to give over the stage for a few minutes to three hysterically funny strippers and to her daughter's rise to stardom before returning for her own eleven o'clock soliloquy. Tynan recognized what Robbins had pioneered:

an integration so smooth, a fluidity so graceful, that the audience was virtually unaware of when one technique ended and the next began, or when one scene ended and the next began.

At its highest level, great staging supports the dramatic ideas in the text.

For "The Ladies Who Lunch" in *Company*, Elaine Stritch did only two things. She stood up from her chair, and she raised her arms—in a specific manner—on the final notes of the song. Simple. Many directors would think they could stage that song. But *when* she stood up, and just exactly how and on what notes she raised her arms (first one, then the other, then both in a very stiff, commanding fashion) made the staging brilliant. It takes a choreographer with a wide range of movement in his or her repertoire to settle on just the right movement.

Great staging arrived in two stages. First, dances became officially integrated with *Oklahoma!* (though plenty of groundwork had been laid by *On Your Toes*). Then, with *West Side Story* and the advent of the director-choreographer, *everything* was staged. Not just the dances—everything.

Play directors are supposed to be able to "block" dramas. That's theatre lingo for setting out the movements of the actors around the set. Some directors arrive at rehearsal with a preconceived physical plot, having decided, without input from the actors, where each character should be and where he should move to from time to time. Some prefer to let the blocking settle in organically by rehearsing the actors in a mock-up of the set, letting them pursue their own instincts. Good directors do both, arriving prepared but communicating their approach without inhibiting a good actor's instincts. That way actors with good instincts make a great contribution, and others get the help they need. But in a straight play, the audience is content to listen, and as long as the director keeps things just as lively as the characters would naturally be, and avoids actors standing around awkwardly, the audience won't mind. Musicals require much more invention.

By "staging," of course, I mean the whole mise-en-scène, which would naturally have to be established in the writing, and then the design, even before rehearsal begins.

Throughout the golden age, dance numbers contributed a plot point to the unfolding story. A crap game, a rumble, a wedding, social politics at an Embassy ball—there was a reason within the drama, beyond the tempo of the song, that characters danced. As this idea became less frequent—in the successful poperettas of Hal Prince and Andrew Lloyd Webber, for example—choreographers found themselves with less and less to contribute, and one-third of the great amalgam of scene/song/dance disappeared.

Which brings us to the theory that . . .

CHAPTER 8

Only Choreographers Should Direct Musicals

*" . . . to which all the individual arts would contribute under
the direction of a single creative mind, in order
to express one overriding idea."*
—*The Grove Dictionary of Art* on Wagner's
concept of a work of art for the stage

More than one director (who can't choreograph) will argue against this theory. And if you were to say that nine out of ten choreographers can't direct, I'd have to agree. Ten years at the barré doesn't equip many dancers with the insight necessary to work with actors or shape scripts. Yet that tenth choreographer amounts to Gene Kelly, Stanley Donen, Gower Champion, Bob Fosse, Jerome Robbins, Michael Bennett, and others responsible for the majority of great musicals onstage and screen. The opposite is also true: nine out of ten directors who can't choreograph can't stage a musical effectively. Unless they can work with a choreographer as an equal. George Abbott could. Rouben Mamoulian "put up" with Agnes de Mille. Harold Prince managed Michael Bennett until he moved his work toward opera in an attempt to work on projects over which he had more control.

A director once defined directing this way: "The theatre is a democracy, and I'm the king." Elia Kazan said about musical comedy, "I think there should be collaboration, but under my thumb." Although he was correct, he was only a director, not a choreographer, and could not stage the musical numbers. *Love Life's* rehearsal pianist said, "(Kanin) didn't have any idea about how to stage the musical numbers." Possibly the most successful director of plays on Broadway at the time, he was unceremoniously pushed aside when *One Touch of Venus*, under his original direction, began to fail out of town.

Producers never learn. They think that successful play directors can handle a musical. Failures in that category are too numerous to list, but run from Elia Kazan to Garson Kanin (replaced by Robbins during *Funny Girl*) to John Gielgud (replaced by Champion on *Irene*) to Ed Sherin (the brilliant director of *The Great White Hope*, who had to be replaced by Bennett on *Seesaw*). The American book musical is simply too complicated. Michael Bennett said, "you have to grow up in musicals to understand them." It's as simple as that. Fortunately, most choreographers have.

Oklahoma! had opened in 1943. De Mille was hired to direct *Allegro* in 1947, the first choreographer in the modern age to direct. (Both Julian Mitchell and Ned Wayburn were leading director-choreographers in the early twentieth century, but staged principally revues.) Robbins directed *Peter Pan* in 1954, Michael Kidd directed *Li'l Abner* in 1956, and Robbins directed *West Side Story* in 1957. By then the transition was complete. Directors who could not choreograph had taken the American musical as far as it could go. The evolving form required an invisible blend of choreography, staging, and direction that only someone with a vast background in both dance and theatre could provide.

De Mille could not see that every show did not revolve around her choreography. Although she had virtually invented the idea of text-based choreography, she was unable to place her dances at the service of the larger structure. The half a dozen musicals she choreographed after *Oklahoma!* were fraught with backstage vitriol. Robbins, who had always been intrigued by acting, and who had been mentored by the structure king George Abbott, was willing to cut dances if they ultimately appeared superfluous. He brought to Broadway the auteur director-choreographer. The final step of integration, in which dance did not just contribute to but was also subjugated to the story, required a choreographer who could stage plot-driven dances, but was also willing to give up dance where necessary. And one for whom "staging" was second nature.

To prove the point, let's examine three rare exceptions: three directors who were not choreographers.

Rouben Mamoulian

Mamoulian directed the stage musicals *Lost in the Stars, St. Louis Woman, Carousel, Oklahoma!* and *Porgy and Bess*, as well as the original play *Porgy* on which it was based. His Hollywood career was slightly more checkered, having been replaced on *Cleopatra* and *Porgy and Bess*, but he directed *Summer Holiday, Laura* (uncredited), Tyrone Power's *Blood and Sand, Golden Boy*, and the film musicals *Silk Stockings* (Cole Porter); *High, Wide, and Handsome* (Kern and Hammerstein); and *Love Me Tonight* (Rodgers and Hart). With

Porgy and Bess, Oklahoma!, and *Carousel* to his credit, there's no question about his ability to direct stage musicals. But *Porgy* was an opera without dance, and *Oklahoma!* and *Carousel* were musicals in the traditional style, before dance had truly been physically integrated. The work of de Mille in both musicals completed the integration of the American book musical, but her dances were done by the chorus in separate sequences (though Will Parker has traditionally been cast by a dancer so he can dance "Kansas City" with the cowboys), and the dialogue scenes to our eyes today seem somewhat separated from the musical sequences. Mamoulian did, as witnessed in existing photographs of his production of *Porgy and Bess,* create great tableaus with large casts for the group scenes. Clearly he could handle crowds. Nevertheless, by the time musicals had become truly integrated, and very large choruses were financially infeasible, Mamoulian had retired from the scene. His last original musical was *Arms and the Girl* in 1951.

During *Oklahoma!* rehearsals, he demonstrated many of the problems directors can create for choreographers. He usurped the stage, relegating de Mille and her dancers to rehearsing in the basement, lobby, and rest rooms. He used many of the dancers as extras in his scenes, having them stand around, sometimes for hours, while he blocked principals. Finally Rodgers had to intervene, and de Mille got the concession that he wouldn't call for her dancers until they were really needed. And he wanted to cut the "Dream Ballet." He was brilliant at creating stage "pictures," but once movement became more fluid and sophisticated, he would have been out of his element.

George Abbott

Abbott's Broadway career encompassed most of the twentieth century. His earliest credit seems to be acting in a play in 1913. At the age of 106 he attended the 1994 revival of his musical *Damn Yankees*. (When the audience gave him a standing ovation as he found his seat, he said to his companion, "There must be somebody important here.") In between, his credits are too numerous to list, and deserve a book of their own. (The only one so far is his autobiography *Mister Abbott*.) However, here is a short sampling of the original, better known musicals he directed:

The Boys From Syracuse
Pal Joey
On the Town
Call Me Madam
Where's Charley?
Wonderful Town
Me and Juliet
The Pajama Game
Damn Yankees
New Girl in Town
Fiorello!
Once Upon a Mattress
A Funny Thing Happened on the Way to the Forum

Certainly Mister Abbott was a successful director of musicals. The reason he survived into the era of the director-choreographer rests with his utter lack of ego—or perhaps his ability to suppress it at the right moment. He encouraged young choreographers Bob Fosse and Jerome Robbins. He supported their brilliant dance sequences, and seemed to like dancing. (Perhaps because he was an excellent, and committed, ballroom dancer.) Though he was a maven for trimming a musical and speeding it along, Fosse numbers such as "Steam Heat" from *Pajama Game* and "Who's Got the Pain?" from *Damn Yankees*, neither of which have any attachment to their surrounding stories, were nevertheless retained under his guidance. Clearly Abbott recognized and appreciated a socko number when he saw one danced. Most of the musicals on the above list, in fact, feature an unusual amount of dance by Robert Alton, Fosse, and Robbins. Abbott's career is the exception to my theory that only choreographers should direct musicals. Some directors are great collaborators, understand dance in musicals, and are happy to see great sequences created by their choreographers.

Although Abbott's reputation stems from the pacing and humor of his shows, Abbott himself insists that this is a misreading of his approach. His "fast-paced entertainments" stem from his belief in simplicity. In "less is more." What he really insisted upon from his actors was truth. Abbott passed on to Fosse, Robbins, and Prince his absolute belief in realism, which, though established decades before in drama, was new to light entertainment. As every director now knows, the actor trying to be funny, isn't. The character *genuinely pursuing his needs* can slip on a banana peel and get a laugh. For Abbott there was no such thing as casting against type, a canard if ever there was one.

It is truth, even in farce or musical situations, that enables the American book musical to capture the emotions of audiences, and not just their admiration.

Harold Prince

First a successful producer, Prince Hal began directing musicals in 1962 (*A Family Affair*), is still doing so as of this writing, and has some extraordinary stagings to his credit.

Let's take a closer look.

Prince worked well with Ron Field (*Cabaret, Zorba*) and Michael Bennett (*Company, Follies*), and was, like Mamoulian, brilliant at creating stage pictures. He is a genius at *producing*, or was when it was a creative job. Both Field and Bennett went on to directing; Bennett had enormous success, but Field, after a super-slick job on *Applause*, faded away. Both choreographers received a great deal of credit for their work, and Bennett received co-director billing on *Follies*. Indeed, it almost seemed as if Prince was going to be a director in the George Abbott mold, seeking out and encouraging the best young talent in the field and collaborating happily. Then two issues began to unfold.

Encouraged by Prince, Sondheim began to work with less "physical" stories, writing more operetta-ish scores. *A Little Night Music, Pacific Overtures, Sweeney Todd*, and *Merrily We Roll Along*, all directed by Prince, had little room for dance. Dances by then had to be part of the book, not just uptempo numbers, and most of those books had characters or plots with few or no scenes that demanded dance. This was not a coincidence: "I want to shape what I do, and the more I use dance the less I am in control," Prince has said in an interview.

And Prince, probably a bit shell-shocked from the amount of recognition Michael Bennett was by now receiving, increasingly turned to uninspired choreographers. Prince's non-Sondheim work consists of *On the Twentieth Century*, a farce play reconceived as comic opera, and *Evita* and *Phantom of the Opera*, two Andrew Lloyd Webber concoctions. Let's see what Lloyd Webber has to say about the form: "I have always felt that staging continuous music as opposed to a music piece with dialogue is the key to musicals. I want to make musicals a continuous musical event like opera."

Prince's oft-stated desire to find the "common ground shared by opera and musical theatre," however, will never be satisfied, for drama is the essence of musical theatre, and singing is the essence of opera. In an opera house, the director is provided little rehearsal time, a cast noted for their voices but not for their suitability to their roles, and huge stages that work against things like humor, relationships, and sentiment. In most theatres opera is about spectacle—the spectacle of the sets and the human voice—and not about substance: the drama. Here is an interesting statement by Stanislvaski, as reported by Joshua Logan during a visit to the Moscow Art Theatre:

> The worst things we have to fight in singers are the singing teachers. They teach hideous gestures and the most ridiculous pronunciation of words. They make the singer believe that he cannot make a certain tone unless he is standing in some strained position with his hands clasped before his chest, shoulders thrown back and chin thrust forward. This, of course, is not true. Tone can be made, volume achieved, whether an actor is lying on his back or his stomach or standing on his head, sitting on his heels or jumping through the air. It all depends on the actor's will to do so. Sometimes singers argue that in certain positions the tone is ugly, there is a different color to their voice. But what is wrong with that? Sometimes an ugly tone or a different color is exactly the effect that we want. If the words were *spoken* in anger or contempt, the color would change. Why shouldn't it also change if the words are *sung*?

Few musicals, including even the obvious—*Sweeney Todd, Porgy and Bess, The Golden Apple, Candide, Street Song*—can be done well under those conditions, and their inclusion in an opera company repertoire, while flattering to the authors, almost always results in an "opera" version, one without a strong expression of the drama in the story.

(To repeat, don't get me wrong. I appreciate all forms of musical entertainment. But what we're pursuing here is the great American book musical—the integration and subjugation of all theatre techniques to the drama. Peter Brook writes, "Anything that diverts our attention from the emotional action is a mask, a counterfeit.")

Prince, in his post–Michael Bennett collaborations, has also staged a revival of *Show Boat*, in which, admittedly, he allowed Susan Stroman a time-passing montage dance. The charming *She Loves Me*, from his pre-*Cabaret* work, is also conceived more as a musical operetta, a small musical with a chorus of only singers. Only *Kiss of the Spider Woman* had a dance or two, due to Chita Rivera's presence as a Brazilian movie star, but those dances hardly forwarded the plot or enriched her character. They were in the archaic style of a 1950s television variety show.

In short, Prince, after working with Field and Bennett, set out to take complete control of his shows, which meant eliminating any material that needed a choreographer. The post-Bennett Prince musicals, and the post-Prince Sondheim musicals, all lack inspired staging. Great sets and beautiful costumes are not musical staging. Actors moving around creates musical staging, without which a show looks static and stolid.

Prince is indeed an auteur, doing everything he can to create the unified vision that makes for a great musical. He has pursued this vision for fifty years, first as a producer, then as a producer-director, and latterly as a director for hire. His body of work is certainly equal to that of George Abbott and Jerome Robbins. But his approach, his desire to eliminate dance from his shows, has aided in the death of the American book musical by reducing its dependence on good musical staging.

The careers of the great director-choreographers are all strewn with the bodies of composers, lyricists, librettists, and even producers. It's almost as if, even in the collaborative nature of the musical, no two creators ever really have the same vision in mind. As soon as the initial, polite, production meetings are over and the work begins to take shape in the rehearsal hall, authors begin to complain—so much so that many directors simply don't allow them to watch the process. In the written history of plays and musicals there is for every clash between a director and a writer, a number of times when the writer was right and the director blew it, and an equal number when the director was right and the writer didn't recognize it. Stuart Ostrow, producer of both *Pippin* and *1776*, and several other extraordinary plays and musicals, says plainly that a producer has to side with his director—until he feels compelled to fire him. Ostrow ought to know, as he had to mediate one of the legendary musical theatre feuds: Fosse versus Schwartz during *Pippin*.

The backstage story was well known at the time: Schwartz hated Fosse's approach to the material. What he had envisioned, a young man's search for fulfillment, did not include the dark and sometimes cynical overlay imposed by Fosse via the framework and the comments of the Leading Player. He hated Fosse's staging, especially the audience singalong for Irene Ryan's number. He despised the fact that Fosse had ignored singing voices during the audition.

(Here I'd have to agree with him. If you heard Betty Buckley sing when she replaced Jill Clayburgh, if you have the South African cast album, in which Hal Watters plays Pippin, or even have Johnny Mathis' recording of "Corner of the Sky," you know there is a lot more value to the songs than the voices of the original cast. Ben Vereen was incendiary onstage, but no vocalist. John Rubinstein's voice was described in a *New York Times* review as a "teeny weeny monotone." Irene Ryan croaked, Eric Berry bombasted, and Leland Palmer gamely thrashed around. None were what anyone would call a singer. One can empathize with the composer's frustration.)

But compromise is constant in the creation of a book musical. In casting, character—particularly the truth of a character—comes first. Though some actors—Ethel Merman in *Gypsy*, Mary Martin in *The Sound of Music*, John Raitt in *Carousel*, Betty Buckley in anything—bring a great voice to a strong interpretation, others— Rex Harrison in *My Fair Lady*, Robert Preston in *The Music Man*, William Daniels in *1776*—won't soon be heard on the radio, but sell their songs through their emotional delivery. In book musicals, you don't want the audience thinking about the quality of the voice, you want them caught up in the emotions of the moment. It's a delicate balance, and the final judgement should go to the director.

Both *West Side Story* and *Hello, Dolly!* received raves for their staging, yet two more dissimilar musicals you couldn't imagine. Thus the American book musical's burden: to carry the day requires brilliant staging and great songs. What the rise of the director-choreographer emphasized was the fulfillment of Oscar Hammerstein's dictum of . . .

Continuous Action

As we know from Chapter One, in *South Pacific* Oscar Hammerstein II began pushing for the concept of "continuous action." Hammerstein was an extraordinary man of the theatre, having begun as an assistant stage manager for his uncle, a successful producer. In that capacity he taught understudies dance routines and rehearsed replacements. In 1920 alone, he wrote the book and lyrics for *Always You, Tickle Me*, and *Jimmie*. Okay, you've never heard of them. His first real success was as co-author of the book and lyrics for *Rose-Marie* in 1924. After that, he pursued the European operetta form until Jerome Kern and his own instincts led him to the very American *Show Boat*. Though the specifics of his contribution—besides the book and lyrics—are lost to the mists of history, he is generally credited with the "staging" of *Show Boat*, what we now consider "directing." As the operetta form died out, he suffered a number of failures, but his craftsmanship was never in doubt, and when Hart proved too ill to go on with Rodgers, Rodgers asked Hammerstein—they were old acquaintances—to write *Oklahoma!* The combination proved efficient, to say the least.

In any case, and to set matters straight, it was not Josh Logan the director who structured the easy flow of scenes in *South Pacific*, but Hammerstein via his original script.

Often one of the ways to go from one scene to another in the old days was simply to black out the lights and change the scenery while the violinists sawed away at transition music, then bring the lights back up. Although this still happens in the modern musical, the more of these transitions you can avoid, the better. They lengthen the show, interrupt the flow, and risk losing the attention of the audience (particularly if you're having trouble keeping their attention to begin with).

Audiences don't really want to sit and watch scenery moving. In fact, one of the dead giveaways that a show has not been directed by a choreographer—has not been "schemed" well at all—is when our attention is galvanized by a slow moving piece of scenery as it glides into place.

One of the earliest solutions to this is the scene "in one," which goes all the way back to vaudeville. The comedian worked in one while the acrobats set up their apparatus. Fly in a painted backdrop downstage and have an actor play a scene, song, or dance in front of it, while you change the major scenery behind it. Possibly the most beautiful song ever written to cover a scene change is "On the Street Where You Live" for Freddy in *My Fair Lady*. If the composer can come up with a song that good, why not?

The problem there, besides the old fashioned staging that an "in one" scene suggests, is that choreographers get nervous. They just don't like to see a character standing and singing "in one." Not enough happening.

And so, principally with Robbins, and then the others, we see the choreographic transition developing. Here are some of the most brilliant.

In *West Side Story*, Maria changes into her white party dress at the end of a scene in the dress shop. Although originally upset that she has to wear it (too childish), when she gets it on, she is delighted. She begins to spin. As she does the dress shop flat goes out and the full stage gym scenery comes in around her, lights change but never go out, and before we know it, the Jets are all dancing at the gym. The brilliance of this is that, while the author has created two separate scenes, the director-choreographer has bridged the two, so that *the audience's attention is never allowed to move away from the stage*.

For *Promises, Promises*, Robin Wagner had designed several different locations in a corporate office, but moving from one to the other required changing scenery. (It was the first time electronic winches replaced stagehands. Following threats of sabotage, the producer hired a bodyguard to sit with him in the basement by the machinery during the performance.) Michael Bennett choreographed the office secretaries to hurry along with the scenery, up and down the corridors of the office, in a stylized movement that *kept focus on the characters*. Although there were no dances to speak of until the first act finale, these sequences produced the dancing girls audiences love to see, without stopping the show for a dance number. This small tease of dancing paid off when they finally gathered for the office party dance that closed Act One.

Transitions also can make their own contribution to the story. Two time-lapse transitions:

Gypsy: When Baby June and her Farm Boys are in vaudeville, they begin the classic "trenches" step, a kind of running in place. They are sideways to the audience, and a strobe light—the flickering light that makes stage actors look like they're in a silent film—begins flashing. As they move back and forth, they are gradually replaced with older dancers, and when the sequence is complete, *they have all grown up!* (It gets applause.)

The Rothschilds: A similar time-passing transition was staged for this musical. Mayer Rothschild hides his five little sons in the basement to protect them from a pogrom. When the danger passes, the trap door opens and out comes the grown boys.

Although these few examples represent the cream of the crop, many more subtle versions have been created by choreographers working in collaboration with set designers. It is still perfectly acceptable to take the lights out on one scene and bring them up on another, so long as there isn't time spent in blackout. Let's put it this way: if applause for the previous scene or song dies down before the next lights come up, your change is too slow. Better to invent the kind of fluid changes that the director-choreographers of the golden age invented for their shows.

One of the most brilliant, and last, of the great stagings was Michael Bennett's *Dreamgirls*. Lighting towers moved around the stage, defining and redefining various locations. These towers were most of the set. Actually, just watching them move was entertaining, but the great advantage was that the show simply never stopped for a scene change. Each scene flowed smoothly into the next.

Critics often compare this kind of staging to the "dissolves" and "cuts" used in film editing. That's a fairly lame metaphor; however, as it is not so much a cinematic approach, as a choreographic one.

When Frank Loesser was asked why musicals are so hard, he answered, "Maybe because people keep secrets from each other. Especially choreographers." Writers and producers need to include choreographers in their earliest meetings, and choreographers need to take an avid interest in the sets, just how the scenes are going to flow together, and what the dances are going to do for the plot.

Another Personal Story

I was once hired to dance in a new musical created in Los Angeles and directed by a man who had directed (but never choreographed) hundreds of stock productions around the country. Remember that once a musical has gone into the library, its transitions have generally been worked out. There is at least some hint in the script of how these things are managed. Unfortunately, this was a brand new musical. Neither the director nor the writer seemed to be aware that as an original production, the transitions would have to be preplanned. Neither did the stage designer. The choreographer, not directing, concerned himself only with the specific musical staging.

One day in rehearsal, two chorus girls approached the director and explained that they had been assigned to a scene as prostitutes, and to leave the stage down left. And that in the next scene, they were society girls who had to enter up right at once. The costume and hair designers had prepared a complete change of clothes and wig. The director looked puzzled for a moment, then shrugged it off. A warning bell went off for those of us chorus kids with a little experience, but who were we to object?

When we began to tech the show, it was apparent that three scenes in a row featured full stage sets, and would take a very long blackout to change. They didn't even all fit backstage. The production manager had to cut almost a third of the scenery, throwing out hundreds of thousands of dollars' worth. Scenes had to be restaged at the last minute. Even then, the show featured long stage waits in between many scenes.

The show never made it to Broadway, and the girls never did make it onstage for their second scene.

And this in an era when the director-choreographer had long before established the importance of transitions and continuous action.

One Caveat

In the replication of existing hit musicals, the scheming has already been done, and, especially given the lack of time in regional, stock, or academic theatres, a separate director and a choreographer, able to work simultaneously, may be advisable. But in the creation of an original musical, the best approach is to avoid, whenever possible, the director who doesn't choreograph. Or at the very least, to stop seeing the choreographer as low man on the totem pole, and see him as the director's equal in a partnership that steers the musical safely to berth.

You Gotta Have Heart

Way back in Chapter Two I proposed that while anything can kill you, only music and staging can put you over the top. As a definition of success, however, you will find a third idea among the great book musicals, where by "great" I simply mean a fair amount of either commercial success, or a passionate following among theatre people across the country. Enough, at least, to find subsequent productions popping up here and there, a category in which I recommend *The Grass Harp*, for example, in spite of its brief Broadway run. This third aspect of the great book musicals which we should consider is . . . heart.

Heart is not easy to define. It's often in the I'll-Know-It-When-I-See-It category. Nevertheless, you'll follow me when I say that at the end of *Carousel*, when a dead Billy Bigelow is watching his lonely teenage daughter graduate high school to the tune of "You'll Never Walk Alone," there isn't going to be a dry eye in the house.

It needn't be so melodramatic, of course. Melodrama isn't a very popular category any longer. It's naturalism and realism that has a current grip on the American culture, though in musicals perhaps highly theatricalized and stylized. But consider these moments in:

Phantom of the Opera: When the Phantom dies of unrequited love.

Les Misérables: When Valjean dies, joining the spirits of Fantine, Eponine, and all those who died on the barricades.

A Chorus Line: When some kids do and some kids don't get the job.

Beauty and the Beast: When the Beast finds true love.

Miss Saigon: When Kim commits suicide so her son can have a better life.

42nd Street: When she goes out there a chorus girl and comes back a star.

Grease: When Danny and Sandy are reconciled, Rizzo isn't pregnant, and the whole gang is united again.

Fiddler on the Roof: When Tevye says goodbye to his daughter (who is going to Siberia to find her boyfriend), while he is taking the remaining family to America.

Hello, Dolly!: When Dolly looks up to her husband in heaven and informs him that she has found happiness.

My Fair Lady: When Eliza finally revolts . . . and when she returns.

Annie: When she gets adopted.

Man of La Mancha: When Quixote sings "The Impossible Dream." Better yet, when Cervantes climbs the dungeon staircase and everyone else sings "Dream."

Oklahoma!: When, with the villain vanquished and Curly and Laurie united, the farmers and the cowhands unite to sing a paean to the land, and, by extension, the great American spirit.

This isn't a list of my favorite examples, by any means. It's simply an analysis of the longest running Broadway musicals. I have only skipped a few for unrelated reasons. (*Oh! Calcutta!*, the fifth longest running musical as this is written, isn't successful because it has heart. Other organs were involved.) We could go on. You should. If you can identify a moment in your musical's story when heart plays its part, you are not working on a stiff. Somewhere in any project that ultimately has heart is the possibility of a good musical.

Which is not to say, as I have and will again, that a "book" musical is the only valid form of entertainment. Though here I will say that in the now common category of jukebox musicals, *Smokey Joe's Cafe* is no more than a concert, though *Mamma Mia* and *Jersey Boys* have enough book to deliver heart.

It may be that in a good production of *Les Miserables*, we are applauding the fact that the cast got through all that singing; in *Miss Saigon*, the sets; in *Cats*, the virtuoso singing and dancing. In the great American book musical, an ovation is, well . . . *from the heart.*

CHAPTER 9

Concepts and the Concept Musical

*" . . . the interpretation the creative director contributes, has
its seeds in, and grows out of the playwright's text and is not
some smart-assed ego trip of a fancy director
pasted on to the text and destroying it."*
—Robert Lewis, *Slings and Arrows*

What is a "concept" musical? That word has been stretched
to cover almost every musical since the success of
Cabaret, which used onstage numbers in the Kit Kat
Club ("If You Could See Her Through My Eyes") to comment
upon real-life action outside the club (a Jew loves an Aryan in Nazi
Germany) even in the penultimate song, pointing out that "Life
is a Cabaret," a universal sentiment (if barely true).

Musicals less story-driven (*Company*, *Follies*, *A Chorus Line*) tend
to be called concept musicals for their lack of a singular rising line
of dramatic action. These three examples present variations on a
theme (respectively: marriage, marriage, and a dancer's life) though
all three have unifying theatrical structures (a central bachelor in
all the couple's lives, a reunion, and an audition).

Performing an entire musical in a certain style (*Pacific Overtures*,
Japanese theatre) or even with a certain look (*Fiddler on the Roof,*

Chagall's "Fiddler" paintings) could be called concepts. In short, call them whatever you want—any well-directed and choreographed musical should be well-conceived in its execution; that is, in its translation from page to stage.

A note in the published script of *Pacific Overtures* reads:

> *Pacific Overtures* borrows liberally from the techniques of the Japanese *kabuki* theatre in every aspect of its production and performance. Freely adapted for use on the American musical stage, these techniques include the playing of women's roles by men . . . "

Search the script of *Pacific Overtures*, however, and you will find *no dialogue or action that suggests or justifies a kabuki theatre production.* That style was entirely superimposed on the story about the clash of Eastern and Western cultures. Granted, Japanese culture includes kabuki theatre, but where is the intellectual support for *playing the entire musical* in such a highly stylized manner? This concept required that only men play all the parts, and Japanese men at that. Yet roles included French, British, American, Dutch, and Russian admirals and sailors, the authentic casting of which would have underscored the East versus West theme. Isn't it disconcerting to hear a Gilbert and Sullivan pastiche ("Please, Hello") from an Asian character playing an Englishman? As directed, the original Broadway production was beautiful to look at—sets by Boris Aronson, costumes by Patricia Zipprodt—but beyond that quite inaccessible, in many cases even to Stephen Sondheim fans, who heard Sondheim's extraordinary lyrics in accents unsuited to many of the characters. The concept did more harm than good to the drama, and thus comes under the category of directorial masturbation.

Sweeney Todd, originally intended by Stephen Sondheim as a musical valentine to the great Hammer horror films, was staged inside an enormous factory, with the intention of emphasizing the theme of man's inhumanity to man at the dawning of the industrial age. Actors who were not in current scenes stalked the catwalks observing the action below. (Director Prince had been enamored with Brecht since *Cabaret*.) The gargantuan set created a cavernous, distracting space around the fundamental box that housed Mrs. Lovett's small apartment and bakery and Sweeney's barber shop. Though great performances equaled the material, the staging overwhelmed even that epic score.

The Happy Time was intended to be a small, intimate musical based on a play about a photographer come home to his son. When Gower Champion was signed to direct and choreograph, he approached it with his personal style: Busby Berkeley redux. The approach that had served *Hello, Dolly!* so weighed down the small, character-driven, sentimental story.

Probably the bravest failure in contemporary theatre history was the idea of using fresh, young, inexperienced actors for the entire cast of *Merrily We Roll Along*. By the time they came to play characters their age in the final scene, it was too late. Nothing from the very experienced and extremely talented Prince and Sondheim could overcome the fact that the Broadway musical simply looked amateurish.

These concepts hurt the original productions. They did not support, but instead interfered with, the ideas in the original texts. While director-choreographers should pursue a creative approach to a musical, it must be appropriate and justified. The vague connection of kabuki theatre to the clash of Japanese and Western culture in *Pacific Overtures*, the thwarting of an author's original impetus in writing a musical based on one of the great horror legends (*Sweeney Todd*), the use of overwhelming photographs and big chorus numbers in staging a story about a photographer (*The Happy Time*) are all examples of a miscalculation in staging a musical, all because a director was looking for something "spectacular" rather than looking to exploit the text's primary dramatic value. If a concept calls attention to itself more than the story, it's misapplied.

As it happens, Jerome Robbins first conceived *Gypsy* as a "vaudeville musical," going so far as to hire jugglers and acrobats, intending to stage an opening panorama of tacky vaudeville acts. It was to be a musical about the decline of vaudeville and its replacement by burlesque. But the authors had different ideas, and doggedly held to the monstrous character and narrower but intense dramatic story of Mama Rose. The story of a stage mother trying to make her children famous, and living through that dream, eventually drove *Gypsy* to legendary status, though Robbins did engineer several beloved sequences: the tacky vaudeville acts of the children, the Fred Astaire tribute "All I Need Is the Girl," and the hysterical "You Gotta Have a Gimmick," in which three strippers each demonstrate their unique approach to the art of the ecdysiast. Reduced to these sequences, Robbins' approach eventually supported, but did not overwhelm, the story. In spite of being the father of integrated dance in the Broadway musical, in spite of a deep background and love of ballet, Robbins always had an uncanny ability to strip a musical down to its essence, and not let any original plans for dance sequences interfere with the dramatic line. A long "Chava Ballet" was cut from *Fiddler*, and the finale of *Gypsy*, originally intended as a nightmare ballet, quickly became the classic song "Rose's Turn." Unlike de Mille, who fought tooth and nail for her lengthy ballets, Robbins direction served the overall interests of the text.

It was Oliver Smith, however, who provided *West Side Story* with the right look. While juvenile delinquents were already in the headlines and the movies (*The Wild One*, 1953; *Rebel Without a Cause*, 1955), there they were realistic. The sight of teenage hoodlums singing and dancing would surely have caused guffaws if the sets had been realistic, the common style of the period. Smith designed light, impressionistic sets that flowed in and out, that reinforced place without appearing to ground the universal tragedy in realism.

When the composer of the musical version of the novel *Don Quixote* looked about for an appropriate musical style, he settled on flamenco, a musical genre from several hundred years after the story's time period. Additionally, the author set the musical in a dungeon, the whole story acted out by its author Cervantes with the help of other inmates. This musical concept worked readily, partly because the flamenco-based music offered far more exciting rhythms than those of the authentic period. The difference was well beyond the musical education of the audience. And the framework of the prison was a time-honored theatrical device— "We're putting on a play here"—that inhabits many successful scripts, including the beloved *Our Town*. Thus two interlaced concepts that worked.

Where does the right concept come from?

The clearest directing strategy I have ever come across was taught to me by Professor Tom Tyrell at San Francisco State University. Although the great director/founder of the American

Conservatory Theatre, William Ball, called it the "Predominant Element," I prefer to call it, as my professor did, the "principal dramatic value." In either case, it's simply this: a director must identify which of the following five values in the script should be given first place in the production. That is, which should the play's overall direction (which would include design, music, acting styles—everything the director is ultimately responsible for) *emphasize*. The five values are theme, style or spectacle, language, plot, and character.

The issue of the primary dramatic value is at the heart of concept. These are the five principal values inherent in every script (good or bad). All must be satisfied, but *one of them drives the play*. To direct Noel Coward with an emphasis on plot would be to overlook the fact that the primary dramatic value in Coward's plays is language. He writes comedies "of manners." To direct Chekhov without an emphasis on character would overlook his plays' strengths. While language was the obvious choice for Shakespeare during the "declamatory" centuries of acting, lately (in the twentieth century) he's been found to be so rich in psychological nuance that character is emphasized.

Although often a text will clearly boast one or the other, there are caveats: to some extent, all five elements need to be addressed. All five should be present in every production, though not to an equal extent. And: a director doesn't have to choose the obvious. (Be careful, this one is dangerous.) Examples:

Theme: The social dramas of the 1930s, particularly by Clifford Odets for the Group Theatre. *Waiting for Lefty.* In musicals,

Marc Blitzstein's *The Cradle Will Rock*, Kurt Weill's *Johnny Johnson*.

Style: Barnum. Although this bio-musical of P.T. had a plot, it was the circus atmosphere and clever musical staging (by Joe Layton) that elevated the humdrum material into a modest success. *Guys and Dolls. How to Succeed in Business Without Really Trying. L'il Abner.*

Language: William Shakespeare. Dylan Thomas. (Shakespeare is an excellent example of plays so full of ideas that modern directors can be flexible, and great productions have emphasized values other than language.)

Plot: Melodramas. George M. Cohan's *The Tavern* was the first really successful meller of the modern American theatre. *My Fair Lady, West Side Story.*

Character: Someone said of Chekhov that his characters sit around talking for three acts, then someone's Aunt dies. Funny, but indeed, Chekhov is very much character-driven.

Meaning that if you direct Chekhov, you'd better have some great actors essaying the various roles. And that's just the point. A director must first choose which of these principal dramatic values needs to be paramount in the production, and then conceive a production that follows that decision, making choices in the creation of the designs and acting that underscore that value.

While plays cover the entire range, many musicals fall into the spectacle category.

The words "musical" and "spectacle" have been synonymous for decades. Lavish sets and costumes began with *The Black Crook* and haven't yet shown any signs of becoming unpopular with producers. The golden age, however, was defined by brilliant staging of compelling stories and great songs, to which sets and costumes can quickly become the worst enemies. This is the great conundrum of the musical. At what point do sets and costumes *distract* from the drama? Ron Field, to his dying day, insisted that Santo Loquasto's sets for *King of Hearts* overwhelmed that show, a musical version of a quiet, touching, and wonderful French film. They were beautiful, though it isn't far off to say that the slight fantasy was perhaps too delicate for the lavish, in some cases eye-popping, sets. (Which the director would have approved in early design meetings.) At the same time, the score was mediocre and the lyrics did not define strong emotional moments.

The vast factory surrounding *Sweeney Todd* and the vast sound stage surrounding *Mack & Mabel*, both omnipresent, tended to dwarf the actors, physically and dramatically. The former was considered a success, the later a failure. In such a collaborative medium, it's as difficult to assign blame for failure as it is to divide up success. But keep this in mind: *A Chorus Line*, one of the most emotional shows and biggest artistic and commercial successes, takes place on a bare stage.

Another issue is the great, overall cohesiveness of a production, the element that American theatre, even more than British theatre (which had a head start of several hundred years), has brought to the world stage. It isn't just musicals that have benefited from the idea of an integrated production. American plays in the golden age boasted a cohesiveness of acting styles with design and direction that created not so much an entertainment as a parallel universe the audience could enter. (American films probably benefitted even more from The Method propounded by the Actors Studio, since American films have brought realism to its zenith. Or the imitation of realism, at any rate. As George Burns once said, "In Hollywood, sincerity is everything. If you can fake that, you've got it made.")

In other words, a great production of *Man of La Mancha* would certainly field an appropriate design (Howard Bay's original dungeon was ideal), and nothing says theme better than the song "The Impossible Dream." Still, one would have to say that *character* drives that musical, and to succeed, one must have a panoply of great performances, starting with the classic dreamer Quixote. To attempt *Hello, Dolly!* or *42nd Street* without a sufficient number of dancers and backdrops would severely cripple a revival. *West Side Story*, for all its difficulty in technique—perhaps the first musical in which the cast really had to sing, dance, and act in equal measures with equal talent—is nevertheless plot-driven. To insure a decent production of *Working*, the musical revue based on a collection of middle-class working lives, one must have a way of communicating the overall theme, without which the material is disjointed and episodic. The musical *Something's Afoot* spoofs English murder mysteries, particularly Agatha Christie's *Ten Little Indians* aka *And Then There Were None*. In this case, do we emphasize plot, à la Christie, or style? If style, is Christie to be spoofed, or taken seriously? (Bearing in mind the valuable theatre maxim, if you laugh at yourself, the audience won't.) The original production fell short in too many categories to categorize.

What was comic opera, and particularly satire of English conventions at the time by Gilbert and Sullivan, is now usually done as high camp. Is it as effective for today's audience? Depends on the production.

While most of the genres in musical entertainment seem lately to depend on spectacle (style), the American book musical depended more on story. That is, the applied techniques, particularly of music and dance, strove to deliver story first, then character, and finally ambience (time and place). Thus in the masterwork *Fiddler on the Roof*, we find a clear story line, rich characters, and detail in the little ghetto of Anatevka. Robbins' "concept" included the physical look of Chagall's paintings, his opening number that defined the village, and a choreographic vocabulary straight from Jewish folk dances. Nothing interfered with story. Kabuki theatre, on the other hand, *even in its original incarnation*, emphasizes style over story.

But concept goes beyond the look of a musical to the format. Prior to the first concept musicals, all musicals featured the well-made play, with songs and dances interspersed, sometimes for good reason, sometimes just for fun. Then came allegory (the best of which is *The Roar of the Greasepaint, the Smell of the Crowd*), Greek choruses (*Company*), comment songs (*Cabaret*), thematic but plotless books (*Follies*), themed revues (*Working*), frameworks (*Zorba, A Chorus Line*), and presentation, the favorite being vaudeville (*Chicago, I Do! I Do!*). The search for unique structures and unorthodox song presentations probably reached its first successful peak with *Company*, which has no story, a conflict only within the theme (Is marriage good or bad? Sorry, no answer), mostly presentational numbers mixed with brief scenes about relationships, a unit set, no chorus, and 14 principals singing songs in and around scenes they may or may not be part of.

Though not a beloved classic, *Company* astounded musical theatre fans and is reproduced still. (Its thin book and 1960s approach to relationships, however, now weighs down one of Sondheim's greatest scores. It is with *Company* that his songs become so much richer in character than the scenes, that his "books" became mere transitional material.)

None of these techniques on their own can be considered positive or negative. Great musicals have invented unusual ideas. *Oklahoma!* was probably the first. As corn-heavy as it seems today, we must remember that de Mille's "Dream Ballet" was nearly astonishing, as was the chorus-less opening sequence, the death of a principal, and the lack of girls in tights. Also, the infiltration of setting-inspired music. Richard Rodgers himself wrote everything prior to *Oklahoma!* in the jazz idiom at which he and Hart were outstanding. Songs for musicals tended to be in the currently popular Tin Pan Alley style. Only with *Oklahoma!*'s western influences, and the subsequent shows of Rodgers and Hammerstein, did setting come to play a part.

So concept has pretty much come to mean anything experimental. Shall we open with the closing? Do we really need a chorus? Can the set be suggestive only? Shall we dispense with a plot? No matter the question, the answer is the same: *look to the drama.* What's the best, most direct *way of saying* what you're *trying to say.* That, and, are we all working on the same story? In the same form? Whether it's a new musical, in which everything has to be invented, or a revival, in which an approach has to be agreed upon (for nothing is more immediate than theatre, no matter how ancient the text), every musical theatre piece needs a concept of some kind—radical, traditional or otherwise.

Reimagining the classics is dangerous. A 1994 Broadway revival of *Damn Yankees* with new orchestrations—some kind of satire on fifties pop—left us with one of the worst revival cast albums in history. A recent *Fiddler on the Roof* with its Jewish ambience removed lost its humanity. But whether it's a new book musical or a revival, a director-choreographer must look to the text for the proper approach. Bringing *You're a Good Man, Charlie Brown* to a large Broadway theatre, adding instruments, adding songs by another composer, and replacing a character all did nothing but obscure the charm of the original. *If it's not broken, don't fix it.* Nevertheless . . .

CHAPTER 10

Revivals We'd Like to See, and Why (By No Means a Complete List)

"What book of rules says that theatre exists only within some ugly buildings crowded into one square-mile of New York City? Or London, Paris, or Vienna?"

—*All About Eve*

Some great shows from the past that weren't smash hits but have a lot to offer could be fixed and brought back into view. Some shows that were successful need careful attention if future generations are going to be impressed. Though nothing as ephemeral as theatre is provable on paper, what follows are suggestions on a few musicals that deserve reviving, and suggested concepts that should augment, but not overshadow, the text.

1600 Pennsylvania Avenue. A notorious flop, utterly directionless, but the writing was outstanding. Needs to be retried, tightened, staged as an episodic minstrel show.

Applause. The pithy screenplay *All About Eve* was ill-served by the updated libretto, and the charming score offers much more than an entire cast of non-singing actors could bring to it. Go back to the original time (1950) for sets and costumes, and the Mankiewicz words as much as possible, re-orchestrate the score for that period, and find out what Ann-Margret is doing these days.

Babes in Arms. Problem: Rodgers and Hart wrote hundreds of great songs for shows that, with the possible exceptions of *The Boys From Syracuse, A Connecticut Yankee, On Your Toes,* and *Pal Joey,* have archaic books. There are two versions of *Pal Joey,* both incomprehensible. But the story is a great idea for exploiting a lot of those songs, much better than the deadly revue *Rodgers and Hart* (1975). All it needs is a clever new book. There's plenty of talented babes around, and didn't *Annie* prove audiences love 'em?

The Boys From Syracuse. Several revivals, and even college productions, have proved this one well worth reviving, but someone needs to do it with two sets of real twins! And perhaps a few additional Rodgers and Hart songs.

Catch My Soul. The first time that Shakespeare rocked successfully. This musical version of *Othello* succeeded in England but had a limited world premiere in Los Angeles. Neither black nor rock was in yet. An entirely different film version tanked. But this forgotten piece from 1968 captured all the powerful emotions of the source in solid rhythm and blues.

A Chorus Line. The 2006 Broadway revival hopefully acquainted many younger theatregoers with the musical theatre's most interestingly staged musical, and, if they are susceptible to the passions behind what *The New Yorker* originally called *musical verité,* the emotion of it as well. Certainly the revival was authentic, as it was a dead-on facsimile of the original. Therein lies the problem. The cast was a replica of the original. But this didn't require them to wear the sweaters and mili-skin leotards of the original. The decision to make the revival look like a period piece undercut the very power of the original show, its immediacy. Bennett's original program read, "the time: now, the place: here." That's still the way to do the show, not set in 1975. And while the black box was startling and original, setting the show in an authentic backstage would certainly save money. The book, music, lyrics, and staging need no alterations. But the boys in the chorus aren't wearing argyle sweaters any more. This goes deeper than haberdashery, however, as we will discuss with *Oklahoma!* (see below).

The Firebrand of Florence. America needs to see what the British heard, a BBC "concert" version in which the book was elided into narration, while the musical numbers were fully performed. Though I am generally against "concert" versions of musicals as half-assed theatre, this technique could save a number of strong scores wedded to hoary librettos.

The Golden Apple. But here's a heavy dance show (and sung-through) with a good score that has been buried for too long, just waiting for a great staging.

Golden Boy. That it was created for Sammy Davis Jr. (who was brilliant and professional) has clouded this show's reputation. Despite out-of-town rewrites, it settled into a strong story and great urban jazz score. All it needs is a leading actor with the brawn of a fighter and the brains of a surgeon to take its rightful place among really good musicals.

Golden Rainbow. Three interesting roles—played by Eleanor Parker, Thelma Ritter, and Edward G. Robinson in the film version (which starred Frank Sinatra and featured the hit song "High Hopes") of the play—were combined to give Steve Lawrence's wife Eydie Gorme a starring part in the musical version of this charming story about a father who wants to maintain custody of his son against the wishes of his deceased wife's family. The original production's angst is well documented in William Goldman's book *The Season*. Put those characters and the story back, however, and you've got a good one with both conflict and heart, and the score is strong too.

The Grass Harp. A light, impressionistic set in a not-too-large theatre might raise this marvelous story and score from flop to charming, though it will be hard to top the original cast that included Barbara Cook.

High Spirits. Not sure why this one had so much trouble finding a large audience, what with a wonderful score and one of Noel Coward's greatest plays, but there were 27 ensemble roles added to a six-character play to little effect. "Opening up" a great play for a musical version is overrated (and, perhaps latterly, too expensive). Concentrate on the comedy of manners, use no more than 8 to 10 dancers in a couple of numbers, and use the overture to stage a "heaven" ballet.

Kismet. The 1950s would never have allowed what an Arabian harem could showcase today: beautiful near-naked women. For contrast, cast the chorus boys not from Equity but from Gold's Gym. Finally, play the script for comedy, of which it still features plenty. (Imagine Bert Lahr, mistaken identity, and a harem.) The luscious score would be icing on the cake.

Little Mary Sunshine. This Off-Broadway spoof on operettas is wonderful, but everyone is—okay, I am—tired of Off-Broadway spoofing the big shows with little musicals. A university with an opera department and a legion of unpaid singers could use this charmer to really spoof operettas with a cast of hundreds, just like in the old photos of *Rose-Marie.*

Love Life. Without a cast album, few theatres can consider it properly, in spite of its respectable 252-performance run. But if the Lerner and Weill estates loosen up, this remarkable musical, which was probably too cold and disjointed for its 1948 audience, could find much future life.

Mack & Mabel. One of the greatest of misfires. The fault lay not with Michael Stewart's book or Jerry Herman's score, but with Gower Champion's concept. He attempted to recreate in too many numbers the film comedies of Sennett. Each attempt slowed the story to a crawl, and each fell short of the film version, the whole thing dwarfed by a soundstage set. Though both stars were brilliant, and Robert Preston seemed to be precisely what Mack Sennett was like, Bernadette Peters has little chemistry for others onstage, and was far better as the cold, impersonal Mama Rose than the vulnerable, naive waif from Brooklyn who finds herself a silent film star. With the smaller but powerful, dark story as the primary dramatic value, and the ambience of the era carefully recreated, this one still has a chance to thrill us. Use film clips instead of trying to stage them.

My Fair Lady. Hardly in need of resurrection, as on any given night it's probably still playing somewhere in the world. However, with lavish productions becoming so expensive, it's time to remember that behind Lerner and Loewe's wonderful score is one of the strongest librettos ever written. Large numbers of chorus boys and girls in gorgeous gowns and striped trousers may delight Cecil Beaton, but they're unnecessary to the show. Let's see a chamber musical version with four principals and ten or twelve others, instead of the 50-plus members of the original cast. A unique, nearly unit set could be fashioned based on stereoscopic slides from the period, and great acting could deliver this great musical into the hearts of future generations. But beware: Americans cannot do believable English accents.

Oklahoma! Revivals of this warhorse have consistently been clarion examples of how not to stage an old musical. The classic look of this show has traditionally been based on 1943 theatre, but the show takes place in the 1890s, and the musical itself is more than 60 years old. Today, an entertaining version might have life-size Brady photographs or Remington paintings of the West as a backdrop, the simplest of furniture, and realistic period clothes, not color-coordinated pastel shirts and dresses for pretty chorus boys and girls. Like *A Chorus Line* (see above), revivals too often represent the period in which the show was first staged, when they need to represent, in modern theatre technique, the period in which the story takes place—in this case, 1890. (In the case of *A Chorus Line*, now.)

On the Town. Two Broadway revivals have tried and failed miserably. Again, the key may be to give up the 1940s technique of the show, especially in set design, and discover a more modern approach to a period story. Casting is a big obstacle. It's not easy to bring both the exuberance of the style and the reality modern musicals require to the Comden and Green dialogue. Choreography is the biggest obstacle—perhaps a less balletic, but still showstopping, approach to the dances.

Pacific Overtures. Forget kabuki theatre, think musical theatre. Cast women as women and men as men, English roles with English actors, Japanese with Japanese, Russian and French with—you get it. And do something about that ridiculous dance that ends Act One. It may be traditional kabuki, but it ends the act with a thud.

Porgy and Bess. Each time it's produced, it seems to get larger. Excuse me, opera companies, but there's a great drama there, and wonderful lyrics, which I would like to hear more than open tones. (English voice teacher: "Take care of the consonants and the vowels will take care of themselves.") Surely Catfish Row would be more authentic as a crowded, stiffling ghetto, and a small cast would bring forth the drama. Gershwin and comrades ultimately chose dialogue where we now insist on recitative, but if it was good enough for George it should be good enough for us.

Pal Joey. A revival could feature a black Joey and an authentic fifties Chicago jazz look and sound, with a white Vera slumming the South Side clubs, the way downtown New Yorkers poured into uptown Harlem joints. A hipper book, a few Rodgers and Hart interpolations ("The Lady Is a Tramp" was featured in the film), and some of their better songs in place of a few weak ones might do the trick, as would a singing, not dancing, Joey. For all its vaunted reputation as an early dance musical, the dance numbers aren't really story-driven, and though Gene Kelly tapped up a storm, there's no intrinsic reason Joey should.

The Rise and Fall of the City of Mahagonny. Brecht's insistence on annoying an audience needs to be curbed, and Marxist dogma—like any other political statement—is only effective when delivered entertainingly. Great drama makes the general specific. We are moved not by a lecture on starvation in Africa, but by the photograph of a starving child. The Weill version, not the Brecht alterations, should be followed. And was there ever a greater false paradise than Hollywood in the twenties? Or a more colorful setting than the Los Angeles oil boom and bust, and the early movie business?

Sweeney Todd. Seems to me this masterpiece has been done every which way but the one originally envisioned by its creator: as a horror film. More organ, fewer extras standing around. Combine a chiaroscuro design with the flickering gaslight of melodrama and the footlights of music hall in a production that isn't dwarfed by the industrial age, in a theatre where we could actually hear the brilliant lyrics. It might be both economical and accessible, and wildly entertaining, as it should be.

Sugar aka *Some Like It Hot.* Not using the film's title was only the first of many mistakes. Casting Cyril Ritchard was another. While Ritchard's stage personality was wonderful (for Captain Hook, or Oscar Wilde plays), he was more fey than randy old bachelor, and all wrong for this Billy Wilder sex farce. The biggest mistake was the one Champion made too many times. He tried to turn a comic farce into a Busby Berkeley extravaganza. *A Funny Thing Happened* would have been a better prototype. First and foremost, put Sweet Sue's orchestra onstage, on their bandstand, which could roll back behind a scrim or down front as needed. Hire girls who can really play instruments. They can play from their train compartments, and be the band in the nightclub. Forget girl dancers altogether; the band will be pretty enough. Find a few better Styne songs (he wrote hundreds) to replace some of the weaker ones. Give Sugar "The People in My Life." The film featured an ensemble cast; in the musical only Robert Morse rose to the occasion.

Threepenny Opera. Enough with the leather spandex and black stockings. I love women in garter belts as much as the English do, but there's no justification in the text for all this S and M. Remember Bobby Darin's swinging version of "Mack the Knife?" Reset the entire score in that jazz style, and place the show in and around a nightclub in Brooklyn, the hangout of the original Murder Inc. Gangsters and corrupt politicians in Brooklyn in the fifties? No kidding.

West Side Story. If it ain't broke, don't fix it. A revival that attempted to transpose the Puerto Rican versus white conflict to black versus white didn't work. The Sharks music is Latin. Their dialogue is Latin. But the conflict is greater now than ever in this era of immigrant controversy. The music and the choreography is universal. Today, with impressionistic sets and without period clothing, this fantastic piece would still be timeless. Two changes made for the film, however, were successful: "America" was done boys versus girls, and the positions of "Cool," and "Gee, Officer Krupke" were exchanged.

Finaletto

"Nothing is forever in the Theatre. Whatever it is, it's here,
it flares up, burns hot, and then it's gone."
—*All About Eve*

Earlier, I defined the golden age as one in which producers were striving to put on good shows, and hoping they would succeed commercially with the public. Producers would do well to remember that *West Side Story*, our textbook example of the great American book musical, was risky because it was utterly unique at the time. Since then Broadway has transitioned to an era in which producers are trying to stage commercially successful shows, and simply hoping they'll be good. The problem with this approach is that "good" and "unique" often go hand in hand in the arts. An approach that starts out attempting to reach the broadest possible audience is by its very nature reaching for the lowest common denominator, and thus lacks the very uniqueness, originality, and innovation that results in good work.

The economics of Broadway, which are not going to be reversed in the foreseeable future, are the primary cause of this. If the trend continues as it has, theatre will soon be in the category of opera, a genre in which very few performances of each production are given to an elite group of wealthy philanthropists.

One solution lies in broader government support for the arts, which is currently a miniscule, fractional percent of the federal budget. That being unlikely, two further answers lie with the media, and in history.

If the major film studios and television distributors got behind the idea of live theatre, perhaps as a form of development (Neil Simon's *The Odd Couple* became one of television's most successful sitcoms), or perhaps simply as an obvious charitable channel given what their immense profits are based on, they could provide enormous resources that could prime the pump of live theatre. The problem is that giving to the arts—as opposed to health, education, Africa, poverty, research—isn't a high-profile idea, and is conceived to have a smaller audience for your brand name.

Historically, for the most part, the arts have been an amateur, and not a professional, endeavor. The sixteenth century Renaissance plays and performances took place indoors, supported by the nobility. Outdoors, "professional" troupes of *Commedia* players could barely sustain themselves. They weren't commonly known as pickpockets and vagabonds by chance. Shakespeare may have retired to Stratford, but he was that rare combination: a genius and a great businessman. He produced his own work, acted in it, coveted his copyrights as much as was possible in those days, did not squander his money, purchased real estate, and left at the top of his game. Most Elizabethan, Regency, and Victorian artists were not so lucky, having to rely on patronage. American artists have been luckier, at least in a brief window confined primarily to the twentieth century on Broadway and on tour, when the American theatre was robust and a good meal could be had for a dollar. But in the history of plays and musicals, theatre has been, most of the time, an amateur endeavor. In the twenty-first century, that kind of production—university, community, volunteer, avocational—will probably be the theatre's best hope.

The problem with that is that unless one can earn a living in the arts, it is awfully hard to make a significant contribution. Actors who wait on tables all day aren't going to have the energy to play Hamlet. Writers with little time to write are unlikely to grow. Choreographers without access to dancers except in tired evening hours aren't going to create the next ballet masterpiece. During the golden age of the American musical, chorus dancers, thanks to the tireless efforts of Actors' Equity, earned a living, while on the West End, due to weak salaries, dancers had to have day jobs. This contrast was, I believe, a large part of the failure of the great English theatre to develop many great musicals.

That great drama, in musical form or otherwise, affects us emotionally is a given in contemporary theatre. In theatre history, however, this is a relatively new phenomenon. In spite of the great poetry expressing great emotions in Shakespeare's plays, and the powerful climaxes in his tragedies, a study of the literature on the period inescapably leads to the idea that his original intention was to entertain, not provide an emotional catharsis. Because his actors—and all other actors from the Greeks to the late nineteenth century—didn't act in the modern sense, but orated their dialogue, speeches, and poetry, it can be assumed that they were applauded for their technique. When truth and naturalism became the aim of the actor, it became possible to truly possess an audience's emotions. As this is most difficult while rendering songs and dances, musicals often still remain in the original context of pure entertainment. The great American book musical is the difficult amalgam of entertainment and truth that was invented during the process we have followed. The elusive result, the combination of technique and truth that leads to the heightened dramatic effect only the combination of music and drama can provide, is worth pursing, particularly in an age of increasing personal cynicism, business corruption, and failed politics.

Interestingly enough, there are now several performance spaces at Lincoln Center devoted to jazz music. Yet very few theatres around the country devote even a portion of their program to musicals. This is partially practical—most have neither the resources nor the experience to mount a musical. It's partially snobbery—many look down their noses at what has often been considered "too commercial" for their highbrow theatres. It's partially architectural—many theatres just aren't very hospitable to singing and dancing and orchestras. But I think mostly it's fear. It's a good deal harder to put on a musical than it is a play. Nevertheless, surely someone's dad has a barn . . . Come on, curtain up!

> *Cause there's nothing like*
> *There's nothing like a big brash*
> *There's nothing like a sassy, tuneful, glamorous*
> *Broadway musical show*
>
> (From *A Broadway Musical*, lyrics by Lee Adams,
> music by Charles Strouse)

A Casual Bibliography

Though this is by no means a complete list, I am grateful to the following authors for their scholarship, and recommend their books to students of the American musical.

Bolton and Wodehouse and Kern: The Men Who Made Musical Comedy by Lee Davis (James Heinemann, 1993). One cannot credit the Princess Theatre musicals enough for their integrity; the true beginning of the American book musical.

Broadway Musicals: The 101 Greatest Shows of All Time by Ken Bloom and Frank Vlastnik (Black Dog and Leventhal, 2004). The most lavishly illustrated musical book to date, and filled with useful info and fun anecdotes.

The Encyclopedia of the Musical Theatre by Kurt Gänzl (Schirmer Books, 1994). In two staggering volumes, the most formidable fact book yet written, featuring not just Broadway but musical theatre worldwide.

The Joy of Music by Leonard Bernstein (Simon and Schuster, 1959). A dozen brilliant essays from his voluminous teachings, two of which—"Why Don't You Run Upstairs and Write a Nice Gershwin

Tune?" and "American Musical Comedy"—contain many wise comments on musical theatre.

The Making of "No, No, Nanette" by Don Dunn (Citadel Press, 1972). One of the first, and still the best, tales of the backstage tumult behind a hit Broadway musical. First, because the author didn't pull any punches; second, because the success of the show was utterly unpredictable, or, as producer Alexander Cohen said at the time, "infuckingcredible."

Musical Comedy in America by Cecil Smith (Theatre Arts Books, 1950). The first history of the form, written in 1950 and still one of the best chronicles of the hundreds of shows that led up to the golden age.

Musicals: An Illustrated Historical Overview is part of Barron's Crash Course series (1998), a tiny pocket book for students to carry around (if only they would) that is deftly organized and well illustrated with many postage-stamp size photos. There's an interesting world-view approach.

Not Since Carrie by Ken Mandlebaum (St. Martin's Press, 1991). Dozens of books carry the same stories of the same hits. This one is unique. Framed with the attempted musicalization of Stephen King's novel/film *Carrie* by a pack of inept Broadway outsiders, it categorizes Broadway's many flops, attempting to explain their quick demise and forgotten moments. If it's true we learn more by failure than success, this may be the most useful book yet written on the Broadway musical.

The Season by William Goldman (Harcourt, Brace and World, 1969). The novelist and screenwriter spent a year following the fortunes of all the plays and musicals that opened on Broadway during the 1967–68 season. What he has to say about the musicals is still relevant and still comprises the pithiest of observations on the art and business of the Great White Way.

Ethan Morden is the author of a number of books chronicling Broadway musicals, from his overall opus *Better Foot Forward* (Grossman Publishers, 1976) to his series, each devoted to a single decade from the 1920s to the 1970s. Finally, his most recent opus, *The Happiest Corpse I've Ever Seen: The Last Twenty-Five Years of the Broadway Musical* (Palgrave Macmillan, 2004) neatly chronicles the recent dumbing down of musical theatre (and America). If you can wade through his precious prose ("the Luntplay of Alfred"), there's a wealth of description, often of the idiocy of producers.

Gerald Bordman is the author of several books on musical theatre and revues and a Jerome Kern biography. In particular, *American Musical Comedy: From Adonis to Dreamgirls* (Oxford University Press, 1982) features outstanding analysis of the various forms and genres as they mutate through the decades, and *American Musical Theatre: A Chronicle* (Oxford University Press, 2001) is a complete reference to everything that opened on Broadway, season by season, beginning in 1866, with editions keeping current.

If experience is the best teacher, then secondhand experience is the second-best teacher. Many of the great practitioners of the art of the musical have written memoirs; others have been bio'd. Here's some you will find fascinating and educational:

Before the Parade Passes By: Gower Champion and the Glorious American Musical by John Anthony Gilvey (St. Martin's Press, 2005) traces the remarkable career of Gower Champion from the sixteen-year-old's dance act to his becoming a Broadway musical auteur. Long descriptions of each show only frustrate a reader who hasn't seen them in person, and one is left with the impression that deep down Champion wasn't a very happy man, but it's a great showbiz story from the thirties to the eighties. *Just Lucky I Guess* by Carol Channing (Simon and Schuster, 2002), a book of memoirs by the google-eyed blonde, includes an interesting description of the working method of Gower Champion.

Alan Jay Lerner's memoir, *The Street Where I Live* (W.W. Norton, 1978). If you don't recognize the title, first go to see a production of *My Fair Lady*, and then read this great musical comedy writer's anecdotal version of three great musicals.

Josh, My Up and Down, In and Out Life by Joshua Logan (Delacorte Press, 1976). Revealing memoirs by the director of *Annie Get Your Gun*, *South Pacific*, *Fanny*, and *Wish You Were Here*, as well as many straight plays.

Backstage rancor is no better illustrated than with the career of David Merrick, told in *The Abominable Showman* by Howard Kissel (Applause, 1993). The behind-the-scenes machinations during Merrick musicals are a warning to artists everywhere that one simply cannot trust the suits.

Four Jerome Robbins biographies—*Jerome Robbins: That Broadway Man, That Ballet Man* by Christine Conrad (Booth-Clibborn Editions, 2000), *Dance With Demons: The Life of Jerome Robbins* by Greg Lawrence (G. P. Putnam and Sons, 2001), *Jerome Robbins: His Life, His Theater, His Dance* by Deborah Jowitt (Simon and Schuster, 2004), and *Somewhere* by Amanda Vaill (Broadway Books, 2006)—cover the central figure of the golden age of musicals. Robbins was both the most admired artist and the most despised man in show business, depending on who you talk to, though in most cases his contemporaries will claim both in the same sentence. These books give you a fair look at both sides. Jowitt, a dance critic, tends to recite plots and criticism; Lawrence examines the man and his methods; and Conrad's book is a great assortment of photographs from Robbins' private collection. Vaill's is the most recent, and the most representative of Robbins' anguished introspection, due to her access to his private papers. It's a cliché, but he was indeed a "tortured genius," seldom happy in his work—which he arrived at via a legendary angst—or in his private life.

Unsung Genius is the biography of Jack Cole by Glenn Loney (F. Watts, 1984). Though structurally confusing and often repetitive, interviews with Cole dancers, analysis by the author, and leads to the films he choreographed are among the few sources of insights on America's most influential jazz choreographer.

There are three books about the ultimate showman. *Bob Fosse's Broadway* by Margery Beddow (Heinemann, 1996) is a small memoir by one of his dancers, rich with behind-the-scenes truths that only someone who was there could portray. *Razzle Dazzle: The Life and Works of Bob Fosse* by Kevin Boyd Grubb (St. Martin's

Press, 1989) and *All His Jazz: The Life and Death of Bob Fosse* by Martin Gottfried (Da Capo Press, 1998) are both full bios, with Gottfried's given the edge for the assistance he had from Fosse's wife and muse Gwen Verdon.

One Singular Sensation: The Michael Bennett Story by Kevin Kelly (Doubleday, 1990). Michael's drive to integrate his dances into the dramatic fabric of a musical, combined with his ability to make those dances monstrously entertaining, created a series of musical numbers that remain unparalleled in theatre history. Sadly, his private life was a bit of a shambles. "I thought I was ready for success," he once said, "but no one is."

Agnes de Mille wrote a number of excellent books on dance. For her own personal take on her tumultuous years, see her autobiography and artistic manifesto *Dance to the Piper* (Little, Brown, 1952). *No Intermissions* by Carol Easton (Little, Brown 1996) is de Mille's biography; deeply researched, well written, and fascinating.

Acknowledgments

Most of the legends, backstage stories, and anecdotes I have quoted here were not collected for this volume on purpose, in interviews. They are a product of my personal journey. Often someone was simply sharing their experience in a dressing room, at a rehearsal, audition, production meeting, or meal at which I was privileged to be present. I can only thank all those producers, directors, choreographers, writers, designers, performers, backstage crew, and theatre friends who passed through my life for their wisdom, and their willingness to share it. And for the time of my life.

About the Author

Denny Martin Flinn (1947–2007) majored in theatre at San Francisco State University, and then traveled to New York, where for two decades he worked as a dancer, choreographer, and director in American musicals as well as in nightclubs, on television, and at Radio City Music Hall. He worked for famed choreographers Jerome Robbins, Gower Champion, Michael Kidd, and Michael Bennett, and many others. He retired from dancing after spending two-and-a-half years in Michael Bennett's *A Chorus Line* as Greg and Zach.

In various theatres across the country, he directed and choreographed versions of the musicals *The Boy Friend*; *Carnival*; *Company*; *Godspell*; *Grease*; *How to Succeed in Business Without Really Trying*; *Sugar* starring Robert Morse, Larry Kert, and Cyril Ritchard; and *You're a Good Man, Charlie Brown*. He wrote and directed the musical *Groucho*, which played Off-Broadway and toured the country for two years. And he staged *Grease, Damn Yankees, How to Succeed in Business Without Really Trying*, and *Guys and Dolls* for the Sierra Canyon Middle School drama class!